"*Honestly* ... ...end. Mike and Kristin Berry ... ..., sharing what they have learn... ...e on the journey of adoption and foster care as well as those considering it."

—Joshua N. Hook, PhD, coauthor ...

"What an incredibly comprehensive ... ...e written for adoptive and foster paren... ...of questions, this user-friendly book is like a manual that every parent would welcome and use periodically over the years as questions arise. Give parents time with this book, and you'll see many dog-eared pages! It will be a favorite!"

—Sherrie Eldridge, author of *Twenty Things Adopted Kids Wish Their Adoptive Parents Knew*

"This amazing book is a treasure trove of wisdom in bite-size nuggets that will help us all understand the good, bad, and ugly of foster care and adoption, as well as how we can love everyone around us and ourselves better. Thank you, Kristin and Michael (and all the adoptees) for answering real questions with intentionality, honesty, vulnerability, transparency, humility, and a whole lot of love, and for clearly providing guidance for our parenting, marriages, foster/adoption support, and self-care.

—Philip Darke, host of the *Think Orphan* podcast and author of *In Pursuit of Orphan Excellence*

"The conversation of foster care and adoption requires excruciating honesty. Honesty that starts from a desire to see others succeed. Honesty that challenges us to be our best selves, especially in our hardest moments. Honesty that refreshes us with the simple notion that we are not alone. I adore Mike and Kristin, and I am so glad they sat with the hard questions, challenged optimistic expectations, encouraged courageous families, and gave dignity to the stories of the most vulnerable—our children. *Honestly Adoption* is a must-read regardless of where you are in the process of caring for vulnerable children. Thank you, Mike and Kristin, for your vulnerability and honesty."

—Pam Parish, author, speaker, and founder of Connections Homes

"With the conversational style and candor we've come to expect, Mike and Kristin Berry have delivered once again. With the wisdom that comes from years of lived experience, they ask all the right questions in *Honestly Adoption*. But they don't just ask the questions; they answer them too. Adoption and foster care should not be entered into lightly. In *Honestly Adoption*, Mike and Kristin provide answers to the questions that everyone should be asking."

—Ryan North, cofounder, One Big Happy Home

"The dynamic Berry duo have written a wonderfully practical guide for foster and adoptive parents in *Honestly Adoption*. They combine head, heart, and spirit knowledge with years of experience in the parenting trenches. Whether you are a parent just considering the idea of adopting, or your toddlers won't sleep alone, or your teenagers are engaging in risky behaviors, you will find hope, encouragement, and practical wisdom in digestible bites. I frequently found myself reading a nugget of truth and thinking of a specific family in my care who could benefit from the words shared. A must-have for clinicians and parents alike."

—Paris Goodyear-Brown, MSSW, LCSW, RPT-S, founder of Nurture House, director of the TraumaPlay Institute, and author of *Trauma and Play Therapy* and *A Safe Circle for Little U*

"As a foster parent of many children, I can honestly say that this is a book I needed when I first began this journey. Mike and Kristin Berry accurately and honestly cover just about every major question that new and experienced parents alike have. This is a book you must have on your shelf!"

—Jamie Finn, speaker and author of *Foster the Family*

"As an adoptee who has read a lot of content geared toward adoption, I believe this is a book for the ages. Mike and Kristin address the questions many parents have, and they capture the hearts and perspectives of adoptees as well. I highly recommend this book for families who want an accurate and in-depth perspective on the foster and adoptive journey."

—Tony Wolf, comedian, speaker, and author of *Serve One*

Honestly ADOPTION

Mike & Kristin Berry

HARVEST HOUSE PUBLISHERS
EUGENE, OREGON

Cover design by Bryce Williamson

Cover photo © manley099 / Getty Images

Honestly Adoption
Copyright © 2019 by Mike Berry and Kristin Berry
Published by Harvest House Publishers
Eugene, Oregon 97408
www.harvesthousepublishers.com

ISBN 978-0-7369-7679-4 (pbk.)
ISBN 978-0-7369-7680-0 (eBook)

Library of Congress Cataloging-in-Publication Data

Names: Berry, Mike (Parenting blogger) author. | Berry, Kristin, author.
Title: Honestly adoption / Mike Berry and Kristin Berry.
Description: Eugene, Oregon : Harvest House Publishers, [2019]
Identifiers: LCCN 2019000378 (print) | LCCN 2019004764 (ebook) | ISBN
    9780736976800 (ebook) | ISBN 9780736976794 (pbk.)
Subjects: LCSH: Adoption. | Adoption—Religious aspects—Christianity. |
    Adoptive parents.
Classification: LCC HV875 (ebook) | LCC HV875 .B474 2019 (print) | DDC
    362.734—dc23
LC record available at https://lccn.loc.gov/2019000378

Printed in the United States of America

19 20 21 22 23 24 25 26 27 / BP-SK / 10 9 8 7 6 5 4 3 2 1

CONTENTS

Part 3: Attachment Parenting

Part 4: Empowering Children

Part 5: Trauma

Part 6: A Safety Plan

Part 7: Self-Care

Part 8: Adoptee Perspectives

WHY *HONESTLY ADOPTION?*

Dear friends,

We are so excited that you have decided to join in this conversation. Our hope in this book is to ask questions and share perspectives that further the conversation and open the door to new ways of thinking.

These questions have come directly from our readers, and they have prompted many thought-provoking conversations in our home. We have been married 20 years and are the proud parents of eight children, all of whom are adopted. We have two sons-in-law and three grandchildren. We were foster parents for nine years and have had 23 children enter our home over the past 17 years. We have both worked in church ministry as our profession.

Mike began writing full-time five years ago, and Kristin left her job in late 2017 so we could work together. Writing and speaking about foster and adoptive parenting has been a dream job for both of us. We are learning and growing each day as parents, and we want to share what we learn with others.

These pages have been a joy to write because our readers have contributed to the content in such a tangible way. We first started writing about adoption because we knew our family was different from those around us. We often felt alone. We began to write about our experiences as a hobby, but the response to our writing was overwhelming.

We were not alone, and others didn't need to feel alone either. Over the years we have used this platform to connect with other families like ours. Here we can share resources, encouragement, and lessons learned.

Adoptive families are unique, special, beautiful, and amazing. Adoptive families are also formed because of loss. Because of that initial loss, adoptive families also have a toughness that sets them apart. We are committed to writing about adoption honestly. We choose to remove the filter that adoptive families often feel inclined to place over themselves. We desire to share the raw reality of what adoptive families encounter so those around us feel less alone. When we honor the hard parts of this journey, we can also celebrate the deep beauty that lies in the perseverance of our children because they are what this is all about. We ask questions and seek answers because we love our children. We learn and grow as parents because our greatest honor is to parent our children, and our deepest fear is that we won't do this role justice.

We also strive to respond to questions without judgment toward those who ask. Some questions are difficult to respond to because they feel judgmental toward the child, parent, or caregiver. Sometimes the question itself assumes an inherent negative personality flaw. Many questions never get answered simply because they feel negative. We will do our best here to rephrase questions in a way that brings dignity to all who are associated with adoption.

Once again, thank you for joining us here.

With encouragement, hope, and humor,
Mike and Kristin Berry

Part 1:

ADOPTION
CONVERSATIONS

1: Should I adopt?

KRISTIN | I want to back up for a second and go back to the moment I decided to adopt. I was a preteen and had been listening in on an adult conversation between my parents, grandparents, aunts, and uncles. I was surprised to discover my grandfather had grown up in the foster care system. He was never adopted. He had siblings who were adopted and more half siblings that his father had later in life. My childlike brain saw this situation in black and white. It was wrong for my grandfather to grow up without a home, so when I grew up, I would provide a home for a child in need. Problem solved.

As I grew older, my understanding of adoption grew as well. I would like to say that I considered all the factors surrounding my first child's adoption, but I simply did not. When I was 24, I became a mom to a precious baby girl. Her birth mom chose us out of more than 50 families waiting at the adoption agency. She liked our house and our dog, and she wanted her child raised in a family of faith. She chose us to raise her beautiful, brown-skinned baby girl, and I trusted she was making a good choice. I felt confident I could raise and love this child well. As I write this, that child is entering her junior year of high school! My understanding of adoption has changed a lot since that precious tiny girl was placed in my arms. She has grown to be strong, lovely, and intelligent. She is proud of her black heritage and confident as a young woman of God. I would like to say I created that in her, but I swear it's a fluke.

My motivation to adopt was much like anyone's motivation to have a child—cute babies! I just wanted to hold a child in my arms. I wanted someone to love and hug and kiss. I wanted someone to tuck into bed at night and read stories to. When I found out she was a girl, I dreamed of buying every dress ever made, and I did. My view of adoption was so small. I saw her, and I loved her. I loved her mom for having her and for entrusting me to raise her. I was honored and proud of every single part of being this child's mother. My motivations weren't wrong—they were just shortsighted.

At first I didn't seek out a community for her. During the first part of her life, she didn't have friends who were adopted. She didn't see teachers, peers, and community members who looked like her. When raising children, biological or adopted, it is tempting to believe that we will be enough for them. And we are—at first. We feed them, change them, love them. As children grow, they need an environment that nurtures their uniqueness and sharpens their individuality. Children need more than just a mom and dad who love them.

Should you adopt? "Oh yes," I want to scream! Yes, you should adopt. Yes, you should open your heart and home to a child! I never could have created the eight amazing children I am honored to raise. They are beautiful, unique, creative, quirky, wicked smart, and funny. They each have the DNA they were meant to have. One has a heart so loving it can hold even the saddest soul, just like her birth mom. One has the cutest dimple in her chin, just like her birth dad. One has a laugh like her birth mom. One has legs for days, just like her birth sister. One has an impish grin, like his birth dad. One has the deep-thinking soul of his birth grandmother. One has the shy grin of his birth father. One has eyes that smile, just like his birth mother. I did not give our children these things. I couldn't—they don't come from me. They are unique to our children and unique to the families they belong to.

Should you adopt? Adoption is the blending of two or more families. It isn't simply absorbing a child into your own family. Adoption is about expanding. It's about growing larger. It's about eating potato pancakes on Christmas Eve because the tradition came with the child. It's about listening to endless stories about car engines because somewhere in your 12-year-old's DNA is an interest in cars that you know didn't come from his environment. Adoption is opening your heart to a child, the child's family, the child's story, the child's past. It's about seeing the future with this child in it.

Should you adopt? Adoption is about loss—and journeying through that loss with this child. Adoption isn't just about the sweet baby you hold in your arms. It's about a birth mother who leaves the hospital alone. It's about a child who will scan the crowd at shopping malls and playgrounds looking for a face that resembles his own. Adoption is about cradling the emptiness of loss alongside the fullness of the child who rests in your arms. Adoption is about balance. It's about joy and celebration and sorrow and loss and then joy once again. Adoption is about sharing—sharing a child with a birth family who may be physically present or may be present only in the heart and imagination.

Should you adopt? Start by asking yourself these questions:

- Can I share our child with another mother and father for the rest of my life?
- Can I support our child as they process through their story?
- Can I support our child when they have feelings of love, anger, loss, or joy about their adoption story?
- Do I have the capacity to find a community of people who look like our child or who share cultural similarities with our child?
- Am I able to remember that the adoptee is the center of every story and that he or she is the hero, not me?
- Can my heart stretch and celebrate a child whose strengths, characteristics, and personality may be very different from mine?

2: Should I foster?

KRISTIN | "I've been thinking about foster care for a long time. I would just love them too much—I couldn't give them back. I don't know how you do it."

She shook her head and rolled a small rubber ball toward my foster son. His face lit up with joy as he reached for the ball. A wide grin spread across his face as he lifted the ball over his head and tossed it with satisfaction toward his developmental therapist, who continued her monologue about foster care.

"I mean, look at him." She gestured to the child's happy face. "I'm just going to take him home with me and keep him!" She laughed, and I put my arms protectively around his small shoulders. With no awareness of the tension building around him, he shook my arms free and grabbed for the ball again.

I clenched my teeth and breathed in deeply through my nose before answering, "Well, he already has a home and two moms and two dads who love him very much," I said flatly.

"Oh, you know what I mean." She giggled again.

"I do know what you mean. I used to feel the same way about foster care. I was always passionate about children needing families, but I have discovered something else. Sometimes families just need support. This little child has a family, and they are doing their best. Have you thought about what becoming a foster parent would really mean for you?"

"Not really…what do you mean?"

Before we decide to foster, we must face the reality of what fostering actually means. Foster families are a temporary Band-Aid while a larger situation is being mended. Those who choose to foster are taking on a thankless and heartbreaking role. They will be at the mercy of the court system, a caseworker's discretion, and the birth parent's capability. Foster parents will fall in love with the children who enter their home. They will hug tiny bodies close and tuck them into warm beds. They will pat small hands as they walk away from courtrooms without the children's mothers. They will feed hungry bellies and pick nits from lice-ridden hair.

Foster parents will calmly wait while a child who has lost everything rages and then weeps with longing at losses most of us cannot comprehend. Foster families will walk children proudly to their first day of kindergarten and cheer as a child scores a goal on her soccer team. They watch in wonder as the 16-year-old young man learns to drive the family car. Foster families will celebrate Christmas and birthdays. Foster families will turn just in time to see a tear leak from the child's eye as they realize their other family is missing the celebration.

Foster families play a role in supporting the family, not just the child. Hours in waiting rooms beside a mother whose deepest shame has just been laid before a judge will open the window to a relationship one never thought possible. As love for the child grows, understanding for the birth family often grows too. Generational poverty, simple mistakes, mental illness, emotional poverty, and years of abuse become intertwined with the story of the child living in your own home.

As foster parents, our hearts are pulled like putty in directions we never thought possible. We love, and our hearts are broken. We feel anger, only to have that anger turned toward compassion. We fight for children and families that were previously unknown to us. Sometimes we win, and sometimes our fighting nature is silenced and smashed.

Foster families learn to open doors to places, people, and ideas we never knew existed. We learn cultures, language, and traditions that make us richer people. We foster because we value the preservation of family and the safety of children. We enter spaces that at first seem foreign, and we often recoil. Sometimes these spaces are unsafe, and the next time we look at the face of the child in our care, we see them through the clearer lens of their past. Sometimes these spaces are just different, and when we walk away, we see that love can live in all types of places.

Foster families learn to hold on and let go in the same breath. We constantly live the balance of these two extremes. We let go as we watch a child leap into his mother's arms. We let go as we listen to the teen tell stories of her father and what life was like before prison or addiction or the lost job. We let go, but we also hold on. We hold on to the parts of the child's story that are too heavy for them to bear alone. We hold on to the resting child in our arms. We hold on to the memory of the one who returned home. We hold on to the sorrow for the one who ran away just before her eighteenth birthday. And we hold on to the one who stays forever.

So the question is, Should I foster? Not everyone should. Some are not able to, and that is okay. Or you may feel the need to in your inmost being. The thought of families pulled apart keeps you up at night. The thought of caseworkers sleeping in their offices because there isn't an open foster home for a child they had to remove plagues your soul. If you hear the pain and still see it as a challenge, if the fear of what may happen stirs a fight in you that you didn't know existed, foster care may be just the place you are needed.

Here are a few questions to ask yourself before beginning the foster care journey:

- Can I put a child's needs above my own?
- Can I put a family's needs above my own desires?
- Can I persevere in the face of hardship?
- Can I keep my cool when caseworkers, judges, Court Appointed Special Advocates, or biological family members make choices I don't agree with?
- Can I rejoice with a mother whose child returns to her even while my own heart breaks?
- Can I find a good therapist, pediatrician, school, and community to support this child?
- Do I have a good support system around myself?

3: Should I foster to adopt?

KRISTIN | Mike and I sat in the car outside a cute little cafe. The rain had been pouring for days, and even our bones felt chilled. We watched couples duck their heads and run toward the warm glow of the front door. We were waiting for a break in the rain as we studied the faces of those entering. We were looking for the young couple who had asked us to meet with them that Saturday morning.

They wanted to talk about adoption. They were full of life, wonder, curiosity, and excitement. We were filled with reality. Our family was going through a rough time with two of our children. We were weary and worn from navigating the foster care system, mental health-care providers, and caseworkers in hopes of helping our children heal from unimaginable trauma. It was hard to remember the hopefulness that started us on the journey in the first place.

"Don't burst their bubble," Mike warned.

"I won't. Let's just talk about the good stuff, okay?" We agreed.

We squeezed each other's hands as we saw them enter the coffee shop. A silent prayer went up, one that we always prayed: "Lord, only Your words and not mine. Amen."

We slammed the car doors and ran through the pounding rain into the safety of the building.

The couple sat across from us sipping coffee and talking dreamily of the child they would adopt.

"We have decided to foster to adopt," the woman said with enthusiasm. "Do you think we'll get a baby? I mean, I just can't believe all the beautiful children who don't have a home. I can't give them back though. I just know it would break my heart. We have decided we aren't fostering—just adopting."

I sucked in a breath and glanced at Mike. He nodded, and the decision was made. We would tell them the hard stuff. We had seen the damage that ignorance about adoption could do to a child. We had been offenders ourselves. We can do irreparable damage when we enter foster care or adoption with ill-advised motives. When we first adopted, we were over the moon with joy. Two years later, we began to foster. We saw ourselves as rescuers, and we didn't realize the first goal of foster care is always reunification—and that is a good goal.

We were foster parents for nine years. In those nine years, we learned that preservation of families is always the objective. Sometimes preservation meant that a child went home to mom and dad. Sometimes preservation means a child is placed with siblings or another family member. Sometimes it means open adoption, and sometimes it just means that the family who adopts the child does their best to honor the biological family of a child who can never again have a relationship with them due to death, imprisonment, or choice.

We have learned over the years that adoption and foster care are never about our feelings as parents. Adoption and foster care must always be about the child. When we first began to foster, we thought our hearts would break for ourselves, but the first time we saw the fear in a child's eyes as they were placed in our car, we began to see that this was not about us.

Foster care is living in the margin. The children are not yours…and yet they are yours. You feed, clothe, comfort, and provide for them. You are not allowed to cut their hair or travel across state lines without permission from a judge. Your entire role as a foster parent is a contradiction and a balance. Even if a child is legally free for adoption, you may still have visits with biological family and caseworkers. Your child may be a ward of the state for more than a year after you petition for adoption.

Should you foster to adopt? I don't know. We are grateful we did, but we would advise prospective adoptive parents to ask themselves a few questions first:

- Can I support a plan of reunification?
- Can I take responsibility for a child without having the authority to make decisions for that child?
- Can I love the child's first family regardless of the circumstances?
- Can I wait for years in limbo before this child is legally adopted?

4: How should I prepare to be a foster parent?

KRISTIN | Mike and I practically stumbled into foster care. Long story short, a friend of ours needed help, and to step in, we had to become licensed foster parents. We had no idea what we were getting into. We just blindly moved forward. Still, if I could go back and make the decision differently, I honestly wouldn't change a thing. We did what was right in the moment, and it has forever changed our lives for the better.

If I could tell someone else who is considering this journey what to do first, here is what I would say:

1. Get educated. Ask around and find other families who are already fostering. Research online. Find the resources you will need in the future. Begin calling local agencies and ask a ton of questions. You may decide that you feel more supported by a private agency, or you may really feel called to work with a state-run agency.

2. Gather resources for your home. Keep an extra car seat, a portable bed, diapers, toothbrushes, and clothing in various sizes.

3. Ask for the Lord's guidance as you take each step. As people of faith, I can't stress this enough. For us, this is the key to all things we do in life, especially things that impact the life of a child the way foster care does.

4. Don't be afraid to pause during the process. Foster care can feel like a whirlwind. It's okay to take a break during the licensing process and regroup.

5. Talk to your children and your extended family. The final decision is up to you, but it is good to be up-front with your family as you move forward. Your children need to know that they are a part of everything you do as a family. They can be encouraged to meet other foster families. They need to know it's okay to ask any question during the process of getting licensed or when you begin taking placements. Use age-appropriate language. Identify a few safe people for your children to talk to. Our children know they can talk to Mom, Dad, or Grandma. (If they just want to share feelings, they include the dog Lucy because she is always comforting.) Safe people know accurate information about fostering, and they know your own family.

6. Remember the goal of foster care. The goal of foster care is always reunification. Your job as a foster parent is to care for the child until the child returns home or to an appropriate relative placement. Your job as a foster family is to support the biological family and the child. Of course, it isn't always possible for a child to return home—this is where adoption comes in. But foster care is primarily for the well-being of the biological family.

5: What difficulties should I be prepared for as a foster parent?

KRISTIN | When we were training to foster, our instructor told us one thing that stuck with me. She said, "You will be investigated. Not maybe—you *will*." In our 20 hours of training, one hour was devoted to preparing ourselves for foster care. In one hour, we were supposed to be ready to handle the difficulties that would come our way. News flash: We were not prepared. Here are a few things I wish we would have learned a little more about before we began this journey:

1. *Trauma.* Children who have been separated from their first parents are experiencing trauma. It doesn't matter if you have the safest, loveliest home on the planet. It doesn't matter if the child suffered abuse in their first home. Children always experience trauma when they are separated from their first family. Always.

2. *False allegations from a birth family member.* You will encounter a false allegation at some point as a foster parent. It happens to all of us. You need to prepare yourself for this. Try to remember that the birth parents you are working with may be angry, afraid, frustrated, or hopeless. If you can put yourself in their shoes, you will come a long way toward meeting them at the point of their need.

We were reported once because after I drove 45 minutes to a visitation and climbed three flights of stairs carrying two babies and a diaper bag, the child arrived with a poopy diaper. I was frustrated and angry.

Then I put myself in the shoes of the parents. They were afraid I was going to take their child. They were worried I was a better parent. They were grasping at details, hoping to discredit me as a parent. Once I realized this, I approached them more openly. I gave pictures and updates, and I asked them questions about the kids, leaning on their expertise. I'm glad I changed my attitude—rather than fighting, I began building a friendship. They were able to get their kids back, address some underlying medical issues, and gain resources. They became our good friends—and still are.

3. *False allegations from a caseworker.* This can be frightening and infuriating. Keep good records of everything that happens in your home.

Document everything. Make friends with your pediatrician and ask him or her to document everything as well. Remember that caseworkers are overwhelmed too. They may have another case that has caused hypervigilant feelings. Address the situation with a calm demeanor and facts. Extend grace where possible but set a firm boundary for yourself.

   4. *Reunification.* This is the goal of foster care, but it is emotional. Be prepared to celebrate with the child and grieve at the same time. If you are doing foster care right, you will care for the child. Even a child with difficult behaviors will leave a hole in your heart when they leave. It is important to remember that not everyone will understand why you are hurting...and not everyone will understand why you are celebrating. Foster care is a mystery to most. Surround yourself with people who will support you, your children, and your spouse as you transition a child out of your home.

6: I'm not called to foster or adopt, so how can I help?

KRISTIN | Not everyone is called to foster or adopt. When Mike and I first started fostering, I couldn't see a reason we would ever stop. The need in our community for safe homes grows each day. Families across the United States are being torn apart by the opiate crisis. Sometimes parents are never able to recover, so the foster care system is bursting at the seams with children who simply need a place to sleep at night.

   I suppose it's not that simple though. Children are coming into care at an alarming rate, and many are unable to return home. When we first became foster parents, we knew that our primary goals were to reunify families and help children heal. Often, children are in care for a long time, and many are adopted by their foster families. Permanency is a good thing, but it also means that foster homes are reaching capacity and have to close their doors. This is what happened in our family. The day after our eighth adoption, we closed our license and stopped fostering.

We breathed a sigh of relief when we stopped fostering. We were able to concentrate on our children and our family. Some of our children have high special needs, and removing the constant court-ordered visits, appointments, and drop-ins by caseworkers freed us to bond with our family in a way we simply didn't have time to do while fostering.

Still, there is a nagging feeling that we dropped the ball. We know many more children need safe places to go. We know parents are still fighting for second chances to raise their children. We know foster families, children, biological families, and caseworkers all need some support.

We can't foster right now. Our heart is still there, but our home wouldn't meet the current requirements in our state. Besides, our home is full. We are aware of the need, but our ability to address it tangibly has changed. Now that life has slowed down for us at home, we have been able to step back from the chaos of fostering and ask ourselves what support we needed when we were still in the system. If you are not called to foster or adopt right now, here are a few ways to support those who are:

1. Driving. Fostering involves so much more driving than I could have imagined. If you know a foster family, offer to pick up an extra drive to school, sports, counseling, or the grocery store.

2. Laundry. I will never forget the time my friend stopped by my house, walked straight into my laundry room, and loaded garbage bags up with all my laundry. She hauled them out to her minivan and would not accept one word of protest from me. She returned the next morning with neat stacks of sweet-smelling clothes for me and the four small children I was raising at the time. I burst into tears. The task was never ending at that time in our lives, but she blessed me to the core with her one act of kindness.

3. Meals. Let's face it—I'm not a great cook. You probably don't want me to make you a meal. Well, you might like my chili (it really is a culinary delight), but since it's the only thing I can make, you don't want to rely on me to feed your family. Meals have never been my favorite time of the day. When we were fostering, I felt like we went through an endless cycle of appointments, laundry, meals, cleanup, and more appointments. When a friend stopped by with a tuna noodle casserole, I felt like we'd received a gift of gold. You don't have to be a great cook to help provide a meal. Call the foster family you want to support, find their favorite take-out restaurant, and have food sent directly to their door.

4. *Respite.* Finding childcare for any child can be difficult, but what about a teenage child who can't be left alone? Or what about a child who has experienced a trauma that prevents him or her from playing with other children safely? Or what about the child who needs medical attention that most teenage babysitters can't provide? You can be that person for a foster family.

Offer to learn exactly what the child needs and then do it. Take the teenager out to the movies or for a coffee. Attend a doctor's appointment to learn to administer medications properly or learn to feed through a G-tube. Providing a few hours of respite will refresh and renew the foster family so they can continue to be on the front lines day in and day out.

5. *Playdates.* My kids remember what it was like to be in foster care. I can't offer them as playmates to just anyone, but often when I share with them that our friends have a new foster child, they are transported back to what that felt like. They will offer to go to the park, children's museum, or zoo with the child. Our kids can be friends to others who are going through similar experiences.

6. *Gift cards.* You can get gift cards for everything! Get creative. Drop off a gift card to a children's store so the foster family can buy new swimsuits. Or slip a gift card into the diaper bag when they visit the church nursery. Money is tight for many families, and foster families have many hidden expenses that we don't often think about. Children may come into a home with only the clothes on their back. One of my foster sons came to us in a pink sleeper because it was the only thing the Department of Child Services could find.

7. *Groceries, toiletries, and cleaning supplies.* Taking in more kids means buying more food and more toothpaste…and making more messes! Collect everyday supplies for foster families you know. Little things like toilet paper feel like a big blessing when you don't have to run out for more in the middle of the night.

7: Do children need to
know they were adopted?

KRISTIN | *Yes.*

All our children know they were adopted, and their adoption stories are always open topics of conversation in our home. They know not only that they are adopted but also as much information as possible. We believe our openness helps our children create a strong sense of identity and self-worth as they grow and process their own story.

Here are three reasons we believe children must know their own adoption story:

1. Truth. Truth is vital in all situations. We certainly do not want to lie to our children, but sometimes the truth is hard. We are born with a thirst for truth and knowledge. It is written into our DNA. To know the truth of where we have come from is one of our greatest emotional needs.

2. Identity. Our identity is what we carry with ourselves throughout life. We may move houses, change jobs, or find new friends, but who we are stays with us. Our identity consists of things like our character, our values, our physical features, and our history. Adoptive parents can be afraid to share the painful parts of a child's history for fear the child will identify with something or someone harmful. Remember that the story belongs to the child. The history belongs to the child. With the guidance and firm foundation you provide, your child will be able to sort through the things that build his or her identity, and they will be able to from a healthy identity for themselves.

3. Trust. You can't trust someone who does not tell the truth. As adoptive parents, we have a huge reason to tell the truth—our children are looking for someone to trust. If they can trust us to tell them the truth about their adoption, they will also be able to trust us as they work through all the parts of their own story. If we lose our child's trust, we will also lose the relationship.

8: How can I tell our child
he or she was adopted?

KRISTIN | Ideally, you will tell your child what you know of his or her story from the very beginning. As we rocked our newborn daughter, we told her, "You are so beautiful—just like your first mother," and "I remember the day you were born and we got the phone call to come to the hospital," and so on. We shared with her every little detail we had.

Some of our children's stories may be too difficult to share while tucking them into bed at night. We may have to save some information for later, but answering our child's questions to the best of our ability as they come is necessary for their ability to process. Adoption is not all that we are as a family, but it is a part of the narrative. Here are a few ways to keep the honest conversation open.

1. Start early. Begin telling your child what you know of his or her story right away. If the child is older, or if you know the birth family, ask questions to clarify. Talk about what it was like to meet for the first time. Ask your child how they felt about meeting you. If they felt scared, happy, nervous, angry, or confused, that's okay. Honest conversation starts early. It may be awkward at first, but you and your child will become more comfortable talking with practice.

2. Talk often. Talk about more than just the hard stuff. Adoption should be an open subject all the time. If you notice your child has her birth mom's smile, tell her. Especially if you have an older child, ask about their first family's traditions, favorite meals, or treasured memories. Adoption doesn't have to be the center of every conversation, but it also shouldn't be the elephant in the room.

3. Share naturally. If you talk about adoption early and often, you will eventually talk about it naturally. Over time the awkwardness of blending two families melts away, and our ability to share honestly and openly grows. Many conversations lead naturally to the subject of adoption. Sometimes the conversation will veer away from the subject of adoption as well, and that's okay too. That's how natural conversation happens, and natural, open conversation is good.

4. Follow your child's lead. Not every child will want to know the same things at the same age and the same time in life. Let your child guide you. Listen to what they are saying not only with their mouth but also with body language and emotion.

Adoption is probably a subject your child needs to process in different ways at different times. My ten-year-old just asked the other day what it was like when he lived in my tummy. I was so surprised. For a moment, he forgot all about adoption. It just isn't at the forefront of his mind right now. His nine-year-old brother, however, is asking deep and thoughtful questions every chance he gets. He wants to know every detail about his birth parents and every detail about his arrival into our home. Both are our sons, but they need to talk about entirely different things right now.

5. *Find a therapist.* Your child's adoption may include troubling details, and you need wise counsel to know how to talk about them. Seek resources and help from others who have gone before you. If you know your child may need some extra help processing their story, find a counselor they can talk with to help them work through the things they learn as they grow.

Here are a few questions for you to consider:

- How am I talking with our children about their adoption?

- What do they need right now?

- What questions might they ask in the future that I can be prepared for?

- What questions have they not asked that they may need to know the answer to as they grow into adulthood?

9: Sometimes I believe a false narrative about our child's adoption. What should I do?

KRISTIN | Do you ever listen to that voice in your head? I know, I sound a little crazy, but we all have that voice. It's our brain's constant narrative about life. My brain tells me I did a great job cleaning the kitchen but only a mediocre job of cooking meat loaf. Then my brain reminds me I don't even like meat loaf, so I probably shouldn't have put it on the menu in the first place. Then my brain remembers that I made meat loaf because my family likes it. And finally the narrative in my head pats me on the back because I'm such a good mom for thinking of others first.

Our brains process everything that happens to us and around us. When we aren't sure of something, our brains often fill in the blanks for us. This happens a lot in our adoption stories. We have formed a family out of many families. We frequently do not have the context to process everything that is going on in our world. For instance, one of our children is an amazing musician. I am not a musician by any sense of the word. I don't have a context with which to relate to our child about music. My brain tries to process everything she is telling me and experiencing through music. I don't understand it, but my brain finds a narrative to help me relate to her passion.

Humans are insecure by nature. We question ourselves all the time, and we respond to our own insecurities with the narratives our minds formulate. When we feel ourselves creating a false narrative, it is vital that we combat the inaccurate story with the truth. We must first say the story out loud to ourselves or to a trusted friend. Then we must seek to find the true narrative.

Here are a few false narratives my adoptive and foster friends and I have experienced:

1. *Our child's birth family is out to get me.* Some people are not safe. However, most people are not dangerous. I lock my doors at night, I am aware of my surroundings, and I teach our children about staying safe. But I will not constantly look over my shoulder to make sure a birth family member isn't following me. Let me repeat: Some people are not safe—this is true. But most people are just doing their best in this world. Most birth parents want the best for the children they love. The truth is that birth families are not out to get the foster or adoptive family.

2. *I am the hero of this story.* When I first began to foster, I sat in courtrooms, doctors' offices, conference meeting rooms, and visitation

centers. I accumulated thousands of miles driving between appointments and purchased mounds of groceries. I put others' needs above my own. It was just the nature of fostering.

I was a nice person and a caring person. I loved my kids and their birth families. I tolerated the constant driving and the intrusion of caseworkers and professionals. All of that was true, but in those quiet hours of waiting and serving and living on the fringe of other people's lives, I began to form an unhealthy narrative. Pride had unexpectedly crept into my thoughts. I began to tell myself that I was the hero of this story—the sacrificial lamb of sorts.

We are people of faith, and I know one thing for sure—I am no Jesus! But in those times alone, I felt I deserved to be viewed as a hero. I laugh at myself a little even as I shudder to write those words. Parents *are* heroes, yes. But the prideful tone in my narrative was as unhealthy as some of my negative thoughts. When I discovered my struggle, I needed to step away from myself and remember that I am not a hero, at least not any more than any other human struggling through life. I am just a person doing my best.

3. *Our child doesn't love me.* A child may scream, "You are not my real parent! I hate you!" When that happens, it's tough to not believe her. The truth is that your child does love you to the best of her ability. You cannot control how she feels about you, but you can control how you love her. The truth is, you can't make your child love you, but you sure do love your child.

4. *Our child might choose his other family.* Again, when the child stomps out the back door and threatens to move in with his birth family, it's hard not to feel threatened by the birth parent. It doesn't matter if the birth family is overseas, in prison, or living in the next town with plans to join you for dinner. The statement hurts.

Do not allow that false narrative to rule your mind. The truth is, your child is processing his place in the world. You are providing security, consistency, and love. Even if your child does choose his birth family over you someday, you have played a significant role in raising this precious child. If you remain calm, loving, and rooted in the truth, you can continue to have a healthy relationship with your child if he does return.

5. *I'm competing with our child's first family.* This can play out in so many ways. You may feel in competition with the idea of the birth family, or you may find yourself competing to give the best birthday or Christmas present. Stop. The truth is, you are never competing with another person. You are exactly who you are supposed to be. You are in the role you are meant to be in. Stand confidently in your role as parent. Your child will see your confidence and assurance, and she will feel the freedom to explore her relationship with her birth family in her own way.

6. *I'm not living up to the promise I made to our child's first family.* Can I say again, parenting is hard? When our child was held back in first grade or didn't pass our state's standardized test, I felt like I was letting his first mom down. When one of our children was diagnosed with a mental illness, I felt like I caused it. I felt like I was failing in the promise I made to our child's first family to raise them well. The truth is, I do not control the child, their academic ability, or their mental health. I am doing my very best.

7. *Our child's first mom picked the wrong person.* No, she didn't. Take a breath and give yourself some grace. You are going to do just fine.

What false narratives have you been living with? Identify a few and start telling yourself the truth.

10: How should I respond to people who praise me for adopting?

MIKE | On a sunny spring morning in April 2002, we walked into church for the first time after bringing our firstborn adopted daughter home from the hospital. We were sleep deprived and clueless about what we were doing, but we held our baby girl close as we opened the door and stepped into the foyer.

You would have thought the pope had come to town. They almost had to start the church service late because everyone had gathered around us to get a glimpse of this precious gift we held in our arms. I stood behind Kristin, and she cradled our sweet girl close to her chest.

People asked us a ton of questions. Where did you adopt her from? Do you have a relationship with her birth mom? Did her birth mom do something wrong? (Yes, someone really asked us that!) Are you going to tell her she's adopted? Why did you decide to adopt a newborn baby? On and on the questions came. Some were appropriate, and others were well-intentioned but wildly inappropriate!

One woman walked up to us and gushed all over us. "Oh my Lord in heaven," she gleefully blurted out. "You two are just angels for adopting this sweet little girl. Wow—saints, I tell ya! I mean, where would she be if you had not come into the picture and rescued her?"

This went on and on for weeks. Every time we saw her, she hailed us as the greatest heroes in the world! At church, at the grocery store, in the park...even as Kristin was walking into a doctor's appointment.

If you feel uncomfortable reading that last paragraph, I can assure you...it was doubly uncomfortable for us. Admittedly, a piece of it felt good. I struggled with not wanting to pat myself on the back. The truth was, we weren't heroes who swooped down and rescued this tiny baby from certain demise. That's just not true. And it wasn't even what we were called to do as adoptive parents. We were called to love and lead this child to the best of our ability.

Have you ever wondered how to respond to these people in an appropriate way? Here are some suggestions:

1. *Keep your distance.* Many people who think you're a saint for adopting will quickly turn away from you when your child pulls a crazy stunt or melts down in public. These people are disconnected from the reality of your situation, your life, and your family. Thus you need to be cautious as you share your story with them.

2. *Share the calling, not the intention.* Redirect those who praise you. You felt called to do this. You're nobody special. You didn't adopt to show the world how awesome you are! And you certainly didn't adopt because you needed to check "superhero" off your list of life goals. You are simply called to this journey.

3. *Ask them politely, out of earshot of others, to stop.* These are well-intentioned people—they're just clueless. (Most of the time, anyway.)

It's okay to pull them aside and ask them to stop saying this about you. Invite them to see a new perspective.

4. Don't be afraid of failure. Your example to the surrounding world will show them what is true and right about the foster and adoptive parenting journey. When you fail, pick yourself up and keep moving. As they say in *Meet the Robinsons*, "Keep moving forward!" Love your child through the hardship of her journey and the moments of deep grief over her traumatic past. You're a mom or a dad who has chosen to love deeply!

Part 2

ADOPTION
RELATIONSHIPS

11: Will our child ever love me?

KRISTIN | In the movie *Annie* (both the old version and the newer version), Annie grows up in an abusive orphanage / foster home. When she is presented with the possibility of being adopted, she jumps at the chance (more or less). She finds a new family, and all her troubles are forgotten. She embraces her new life, and in the grand finale, everyone sings, dances, and celebrates her adoption. Hmm…no wonder adoptive and foster parents are confused when they open their home to a child who is less than pleased to be a part of their lives.

One of our daughters came to live with us when she was three years old. I loved her instantly, and I wanted to hug her and kiss her sweet face and snuggle with her and dress her up…but she wanted nothing to do with me. My home was safe and my hugs were genuine, but she was not ready to receive that. I longed for her to love me back or at least show love in a way I could understand.

Over the years, her trust for me grew. I really did provide food like I said I would. I didn't hit or hurt her, and I tucked her in every night, even when she turned her back to me. One day when she was 11, much to my surprise, she came up behind me and hugged me. I froze, not wanting to disturb the moment.

Many adopted children have lost trust in others, and they often don't know how to show love. They have lost the vulnerability it takes to let an adult know they need them, trust them, and even love them. Love is not as simple as falling. Love takes time, and it goes hand in hand with trust. Your child can love you back. Your child probably will love you back. It's going to take time, determination, and a lot of patience on your part as you lead your child to accept others, build healthy relationships with them, receive love from them, and express love in return.

- Love takes time.
- Love takes patience.
- Love is learned through example.

12: Will I ever love our child?

KRISTIN | Relationships are tough—even parent/child relationships. No one wants to admit they struggle to love their child, but it's important to address it here so we can move forward from the shame.

Loving another person doesn't always happen all at once. Love grows over time. Is it true that sometimes parents (biological, step, foster, or adoptive) feel an overwhelming love immediately upon seeing the child for the first time? Yes, of course. But that feeling of fierce love sometimes starts as a lukewarm emotion. This confusing feeling can be compounded when a child arrives long after the infant and toddler years, is extremely fussy, spends a significant amount of time in the hospital, and so on.

What do we do when we feel this alarming sense of not-quite-love for the child who has been entrusted to us?

1. Find a trusted friend to share with. Often just talking about the feeling opens the door that has been closed to that hesitant feeling of love.

2. Make a plan. What are some things you admire about the child? Say these things out loud to your friend and others around you: "Doesn't our daughter have the most brilliant smile?" or "I'm so proud of our daughter for working so diligently at school this year." This may sound silly, but there is really something to declaring your love verbally. Tell your child something every day that you like about them. Point out their strengths. This will go a long way to building the trust your child has for you as well.

3. Find a way to show affection in a way that is comfortable for both of you. When a child is uncomfortable with affection, it can feel like a barrier to developing a genuine sense of love for one another. The refusal to hug can feel like a rejection. Even when we know where our child is coming from, it can feel like a wall is between us. It's okay that you and your child aren't comfortable with hugging.

Find a special way to connect. High-five before they get on the bus. If that's too much, high-one (like a high-five but with one finger). If the child is smaller, try swaddling or carrying him in a child carrier. One of my toddlers could not hug face-to-face but relaxed when he was in the backpack carrier.

4. Be patient and persistent. You and your child have a lifetime to grow into a loving relationship.

13: Will our child and I ever have a healthy relationship?

KRISTIN | Parenting doesn't end at 18. You may develop a healthy relationship when they are very small, or it may take longer. You may have seasons of life when you feel that you will never connect in a healthy way. (The teenage years, for instance!) Remember that there is no end to parenting. You are in a marathon, not a sprint. Build your relationship slowly and carefully.

When you lose the connection, try again. When you mess up as a parent, try again. When your child pushes you away, don't lose hope. Model appropriate and healthy relationships in front of your child. Talk openly with your child as they get older about your desires for your family. Our children may be dealing with feelings of abandonment that cause them to put a wall up in front of those who love them the most. Sometimes our children firmly believe we are going to leave them or we don't want them. Remember to leave no room for thoughts like these to grow. Be patient, set a good example, and be patient again. Yes, you can have a healthy relationship with your child.

- Connect with your children intentionally.

- Invite your child to connect with you, but don't expect anything in return. Just keep the door open.

- Model healthy relationships in your own life. Your child will learn through your example.

14: Will I be able to love our children equally?

MIKE | I remember the morning very clearly. It was early spring in Indiana. Tiny leaves were beginning to appear on the trees. The morning air was still crisp, a holdover from the harsh winter we had just survived. By the time I made it to the coffee shop to meet my friend, the sun had already melted away the light layer of frost that had adorned the earth the night before.

My friend had tears in his eyes as he sat down in front of me at the tiny table in the corner of the restaurant. "Mike, I just don't know if we can do this," he said to me through a tone of exhaustion. He looked to the side, shifting his gaze from me, wiping tears away, and shaking his head in shame. After what seemed like hours of silence, I finally asked him a question: "What are you afraid of?"

"How did you know I'm afraid of something?"

"Because," I replied, "everyone who does this has a measure of fear coursing through their veins at one point or another on this journey. I was scared to death the first time we adopted."

"I'm just worried that Sara and Mason will feel pushed aside and not loved if we spend a lot of time focusing on the kids that are about to come into our home. The case manager told us they have been through a lot. It's gonna take a lot of our time. I'm just afraid my kids won't feel like we love them as much. Or if we start spending special time with Sara and Mason, maybe our new kids will feel pushed aside."

His questions were valid and not uncommon. Here are some answers I shared with him that morning:

1. The importance of awareness. There is value in being aware of something. You are aware you may end up spending a lot of time working with the children you foster or adopt, so when the time comes, you're likely to take action to make sure all your kids feel loved.

2. *Turn awareness into action.* Choose every day to blanket all your children with love and affection. Several years ago, we had some acquaintances over for dinner during the holidays. As we sat around our dining room table, the husband asked us, "With all of these children, how do you show each one individual attention?"

We simply answered, "Well, we just do."

3. *Be intentional.* We turn our awareness into action every single week. We make sure each of our children gets individualized attention every week. It comes down to intentionality. Take one child with you to the grocery store or help your child with his homework in a quiet room alone. What you are intentional about is what is most important to you.

4. *Recognize your infinite space for love.* Our ability to love doesn't depend on the space in our hearts. As human beings, we have plenty of space in our hearts. We were created by love to love. Loving one person does not lessen our love for another.

5. *Remember love is a choice.* Will you love your adopted children the same as you do your biological children? I'll answer the question with a question: What will you choose to do? You have the capacity in your heart to love all children. But only you can choose to love.

15: How can we keep our forever children from feeling neglected?

MIKE | (We use the term "forever" children to identify the children who are staying in our home forever either because they are biologically related or legally adopted.)

Anytime you are caring for children who have come to your home from traumatic situations, there will be difficulties, and you may spend a lot of time dialed into their needs. Sometimes their behaviors will dominate your time. You may need to find new ways to focus on your forever children as well.

You need to be intentional about spending adequate time with each of your children. Just this afternoon, Kristin and I were going over our schedule for the next few days. She told me she was planning a day trip to see her brother and his family in Ohio, and she would be taking our second-oldest son with her. He needed some special time away from his brothers. Simple planning can make a profound difference in balancing your relationship with all your children.

- *Plan special time with each of your children.* This doesn't have to be a weekend away—it can be a quick trip to the grocery store with just one child.

- *Be open.* Create a safe space for your children to discuss their fears and concerns openly. Your listening ear will help ease the many transitions that take place in the home of foster and adoptive families.

- *Create a safe physical space.* Your children should have a space that belongs to just them. Each child should have a bedroom, bed, dresser, and shelf that are just theirs.

- *Create a safe emotional space.* Each child should have a time and place they can feel their emotions properly. This may be time away from the house or a few minutes alone with Mom or Dad each night as they are getting tucked into bed.

16: How can we prepare our forever children before fostering?

MIKE | When we first began our journey, we did so through private adoption. But just two years later, our home became open to foster placements. At the time, our firstborn daughter was only two years old. We had simple conversations with her, but she really didn't understand what we were doing.

However, in 2007, we had three forever children who had grown accustomed to having their own spaces in our house, and we suddenly added two foster children. "You want me to do what?" our kids asked when a ten-year-old boy and his baby sister came to live with us. They arrived in the middle of the night while our children were asleep. Imagine waking up to discover you had been moved around in your sleep and a stranger was sleeping in your room. We learned a lot from that experience and what to do differently the next time.

1. *Prepare for the inevitable.* Prepare as much as you possibly can. Tell your children what might happen and talk through scenarios with them.

2. *Communicate.* Talk out every angle and listen to your children's deepest thoughts on the subject. Your goal is to open clear lines of communication before you begin the process. Create a safe space for your children to ask questions and process the answers. Communicate with each other and with your forever children. Allow them to ask questions, and discuss this topic as a family.

3. *Give them time.* Foster care is not something you should rush into. Your forever children need time to process this decision, adjust their thinking, and build their understanding. If you're considering this journey, make sure you give it a lot of time and a lot of space so you and your forever children have plenty of time to explore every angle, communicate with one another, and proceed in as much unity as possible.

4. *Try to arrange a visitation.* This isn't always possible, but if you have a chance, meet the children who are coming into your home and allow the children to meet one another as well.

5. *Consider making a covenant.* A covenant is a promise and a commitment. Promise only what you can guarantee. For instance, "I promise you that even when we are fostering, I will make special time for just the two of us once a month," or "I can't promise to know how this journey will go, but I do promise to always listen to how you are feeling without judgment."

6. *Guard their space.* Provide a sacred space for your children that you guard on their behalf. This could be their bedrooms, a special corner in the playroom, or a clubhouse. As you prepare your forever children to begin fostering, it's critical that you intentionally create

guarded spaces for them before you begin the process. Take some time to clear out a space for your forever children to keep books, keepsakes, or other special possessions.

17: How should we explain foster care to our forever children?

KRISTIN | Foster care is a temporary solution to a much larger problem. A child enters foster care only after it is determined that his or her parents are not able to safely care for the child. The goal of foster care should always be reunification. We foster parents must always assist in the preservation of biological family to the best of our ability. We are entrusted with the care of a child full-time, just as if he or she were our own. This can be a delicate and confusing balance for adults and so much more for children. As you begin to explain to your child what is happening, it is important to keep a few things in mind:

1. *Determine your child's maturity level.* You know your child best, and you know what they are ready to understand. If your child is small, you may say, "Janie is coming to stay with us for a while. She will sleep here and eat here." An older child may understand, "Janie needs to stay with us for a while. Her mom and dad aren't able to care for her right now. We need to be a family to her while her mom and dad get some things worked out."

2. *Include the child in planning.* Invite your child to think of some things the new child will need while they are in the home. Your forever children will understand more about what is happening when they are included in preparing bedrooms, buying an extra toothbrush, or setting an extra plate at the table.

3. *Be open but keep the child's information private.* If you know that the child has a change of case plan, tell your other children. If you know that the child's mom just failed a drug screen, keep that information private. Use your best judgment. Ask yourself what you would need to know if you were in your forever child's position. Ask yourself what you would want kept private if you were in your foster child's place.

18: How can we prepare our forever children to share with foster children?

KRISTIN | We begin learning to share almost from birth. We share our toys when friends come over. We learn to ask politely for the green crayon in preschool, and by elementary school we know that we can't have the teacher's undivided attention. However, sharing with a foster child is tricky. Having a child come into your home sharing toys, a table, a bedroom, and even Mom and Dad can send any child into a tizzy. It is important that we prepare our children to share with a new child in the home.

1. Determine what your child doesn't have to share. Some things are off limits. A child's bed, favorite toy, or special blanket is not something that should be shared with another child. Before you begin fostering, talk with your child about what things are theirs alone. Children need to have a sense of power in making their own choices.

2. Determine what will be shared. You will have to share Mom's and Dad's time. You will have to share the family television. Talk with your children about some of the things they will be expected to share with the new child.

3. Give them space to think about what this might be like. Practice what will happen if a foster child tries to take their special blanket. Also practice what will happen if the forever child doesn't want to share with the new child and how they will be able to work past that.

4. Encourage your child to put himself or herself in the shoes of the new child. What would it feel like to come into a strange home and not have anything of your own? How can your child help any foster children who enter your home and make them feel welcome?

19: What should I do if my forever children are resistant to fostering?

KRISTIN | My children don't like to brush their teeth or eat vegetables. Last year when we moved to a new house, one of my children had a pouting standoff that lasted six months! When I left my job at a church they loved, they grieved. My children don't like some of the choices Mike and I make for our family, and we respect that. Children need to feel safe to express their opinions and concerns. However, adults make decisions for the family. As the parents, we do our best to make decisions that are healthy and good for our children. If we choose to be a foster family, it is ultimately our choice. So what do we do if our children are resistant to our choice?

1. Listen. Often when we are resistant to a new idea, it is because we feel unheard. There is so much power in being able to verbally work through our hesitations, concerns, and questions. We can offer our children a listening ear.

2. Answer questions to the best of your ability. You may not know all the answers, but be honest about that too.

3. Stick with your decision. Children can feel out of control when parents do not seem confident about their choices. Be truthful if you are unsure about something, but make sure your children feel your confidence as well.

20: What should I do if I'm fostering or adopting out of birth order?

MIKE | Birth order is the order in which children are born. In a typical family, the oldest child will always be the oldest and so on. The only additions will be younger children, and the only change placement will be if a youngest child becomes a big brother or sister. In foster care and adoption, sometimes birth order isn't something that can be maintained.

Many adoption experts consider adopting out of birth order to be detrimental to the development of all children involved. However, sometimes birth order must be disrupted because a child needs a place to live.

Our first child became a big sister and a little sister at the age of two. Later we adopted two teenage sisters, and she eventually became our fourth oldest even though she was the first to be adopted. We feel grateful that our child feels she is in the exact place in our family that she was meant to be. This isn't the case for all children, so it's important to know your child and set boundaries accordingly.

If you find yourself faced with the decision to adopt out of birth order, there are a few ways you can be prepared. Over the past 15 years, our children have jockeyed birth-order positions several times. Each time we've learned a thing or two. Here's what I suggest:

1. Communicate, communicate, communicate. As you bring children into your home, communication is key. You must begin the conversation with your children about what is about to happen. Let them know that you are aware that things will be different. Explain how you will help them feel comfortable. Disrupting birth order changes things.

2. Give permission to express. As you talk about a potential jockeying of birth-order position, give your forever children permission to express their views and opinions. The final decision is yours, but you must listen to your children (who own a share in the home). If possible, give this a lot of time and space. This is not the topic of conversation to bring up casually over dinner and wrap up by the time dessert is served.

3. Answer as many questions as possible from your forever children. Expect questions and welcome them. Allow them to spend as much time as possible asking as many questions as they want to. They may want to know if they are losing their bedroom, if they will lose time on the Xbox, if they have to share their clothes. Your older children may have more serious questions: Does this mean you won't be able to go on your special weekly coffee date like you had been doing? What happens when this new kid starts driving? Will your children have to share the car with them?

4. Commit yourself to a healthy balance as a parent. Adding children to your home stretches your time and energy. Keep yourself healthy and give each of your children the time and attention they need.

5. Remember your forever children. As your family grows and the birth order shifts, be intentional about spending time with all your children. Be mindful of those who are always going to be a part of your family.

21: How will fostering change our forever kids?

MIKE | If a child comes from a traumatic situation to live with you, will he or she be a bad influence on your other children? Will she cause such a disruption that your other children experience secondary trauma?

I understand where questions like these come from, but I also know they are driven by a lot of myths surrounding the foster care journey. The media have often portrayed foster children as bad kids who have done bad things or troubled children who wreak havoc on a family. Children who have come from significant trauma can behave in extreme ways. Understanding this and becoming equipped to handle these behaviors can make all the difference for your forever children.

In his book *Reframing Foster Care*, our good friend Jason Johnson shares an important principle that anyone who is considering foster care should understand before they enter the journey:

> As parents we are naturally inclined to want to isolate and insulate our kids from things that are hard…I used to be concerned about the effects that bringing kids from foster care into our home would have on our bio kids. Now, after the fact, I'm more concerned about the effects of NOT bringing them into our home. This has given our daughters a gift that we (as mom and dad) would have never been able to give them on our own.

That's the healthiest perspective we can have going into foster care. This is an opportunity for our forever children to learn compassion, kindness, and servanthood. This is a chance to teach our children about putting others first. Foster care teaches our families to focus on others.

Our hope and prayer has always been, "May this change our children for the better." And it truly has! If you are worried about how your children will be affected by bringing other children into your home, here are a few things to keep in mind:

- *We are preparing our children to live in the world.* They will encounter others who are not like their own family. They will be challenged to see from a new perspective, and they will have to make decisions about the type of person they will become. They will begin this journey of self-discovery in the security of their own home when the home is open to welcoming others.

- *Keep in connection with your children.* Discuss any behaviors that are concerning. Remind your children often what your values are as a family.

- *Encourage empathy.* Teach your children to have empathy with children who enter your home. This empathy will serve them well throughout life.

22: Why is open adoption becoming more popular?

KRISTIN | When a child is adopted, the families create a post-adoption agreement. (The document may have a different name in your state.) This agreement addresses the amount of contact the families will have and what information they will share with one another. In a closed adoption, all information is kept private. In an open adoption, families share openly, exchange correspondence, and even visit.

When we first adopted, we chose to abide by the precautions set forth by our adoption agency. We kept a post office box in a different town and kept our last name out of any documentation. We didn't use any identifying information in our conversations and never allowed photos to be taken of us in locations that might allude to the location of our home.

On the day our daughter was born, we paced in the waiting room for hours. Finally, the nurse called us to the back of the newborn nursery, and we saw the most beautiful baby girl swaddled tightly in her tiny bassinet. The nurse introduced himself and handed her to us. His last name was also Berry, and we laughed and said, "That's our name too!" We immediately realized our mistake. We had not planned on giving our name to anyone, but two minutes into this adoptive parenting thing, we had already blown it.

As we cradled that tiny child in our arms, love for her and for her first mom filled my heart to the point of bursting. All at once, I wanted to know her. I wanted to hug her and cry with her and promise her I would love and protect her child with my whole being.

Not all adoption situations are like ours. And sometimes we must be careful of people. All people. Sometimes the people we should be able to trust—teachers, mail carriers, ministers, and even our own relatives—are not safe.

My preschool teacher taught us the golden rule—"Do unto others as you would have them do unto you." In other words, ask yourself, "If I were in this situation, how would I want to be treated?" I find that this concept applies to our lives as foster and adoptive parents. We often appear to have the upper hand—we have custody of the child, we make the day-to-day decisions for the child, a judge ordered for that child to be placed in our home, and so on. To the birth family, we are intimidating. Many times our child's birth family does not approach us because they feel they are not welcome or that they do not measure up. In contrast, birth families may approach us in a way that feels demanding. When we allow ourselves to sit for a moment in the emotions of our child's birth family, it is easy to begin to understand their perspective. I ask myself how I would feel if I were in their position.

I also try to put myself in our child's shoes. If I were an adoptee, what would I want to know about my first family? What would I want my relationship with them to be like? If I were the birth mom, I would want to know that our child is adored, loved, safe, and happy. I would dream of hugging our child and hearing her voice. My friends who are birth mothers have told me they dream about their child. They marked birthdays and special events silently in their own hearts, alone.

When our daughter was born, I took thousands of pictures. This was back in the days of film! I dropped off rolls and rolls of film and then waited with anticipation for two days to get the pictures back of the child I could see with my own two eyes every day. New parents are silly. After I put her to bed, I would take the pictures and spread them out around me on the living room floor and pick out the very best for her first mom. I wanted her to have one of every facial expression. I wanted to breathe into each picture the life we lived. My heart's desire was for our daughter's mom to feel comfort. I could only imagine her worry, fear, or regret as I captioned each photo and placed them in an envelope for her. It was and still is my desire for my daughter and her first mom to know each other one day.

Years later we sat in an interview with two grandmothers who had been given the impossible responsibility of finding new parents for their two grandsons. They interviewed several couples, and when it was our turn to answer their questions, they asked if we would still allow them to be in the boys' lives. Without hesitation we both said yes. Who wouldn't want to have two more grandparents around to love and spoil and dote on the children? We were chosen to adopt the boys! Years later as we sat around the dinner table with these special ladies, they told us their decision was made when we said we wanted the children to know them. These special ladies not only love their two biological grandsons—they love all our children and us too.

Open adoption can mean all types of things. It can mean sharing pictures, phone calls, and conversations. It can mean cookouts and playdates at the park. It can also mean sharing in the details of life intimately. Holding each other's hands at a funeral. Rejoicing at a wedding. Hugging in celebration at the birth of another generation.

Not all connections are good and healthy, but those that are remain priceless for you, your child, and your child's first family. So consider these steps:

- Determine whether the relationship is safe.

- Make a plan that honors the birth family as well as the adoptive family in a way that is healthy for the child.

- Honor your promises to your child and to your child's birth family.

23: How should we prepare to meet our child's birth parents for the first time?

KRISTIN | No matter the circumstance, we believe that establishing a healthy relationship with our child's biological family members is essential to helping our child grow and develop. Your child's identity is partly his or her DNA. Whether this natural connection has been severed by choice or circumstance, we cannot deny a child's connection to biological family.

Meeting each of our children's birth parents for the first time was exciting, nerve-racking, and enlightening. We have met people at a prison, at a local park, at a fast-food restaurant, and in the waiting room at family court. We have even met a birth family by accident while out in the community. Sometimes we have a long time to prepare (14 years in the case of our daughter), and sometimes we have no time to prepare (one minute when a caseworker initiated an impromptu meeting).

Even though we may have felt nervous during the first meeting, we have learned that the relationship is about the child, not about us. We must take initiative to help the meeting go well. Here are a few steps to remember when you are meeting for the first time:

1. Assume the best. Not all meetings will go well, but most do. Go into the first meeting assuming the best about the other person. Seek to understand where they are coming from. Lay aside what you think you know and meet this person with fresh eyes. Look for common ground.

2. Ask yourself how the other person may be feeling. What do they think of you? What are their fears, joys, sorrows? If you were in their position, what would you want from the foster or adoptive parent? What would you want to know about your child?

3. Don't let unconfirmed fear control you. Sometimes we should be afraid. Fear is often what preserves our lives. Fear tells us to seek shelter during a tornado. Fear causes us to swerve out of the way of an oncoming car. Unchecked fear can also control us in irrational ways. Ask yourself, "Should I be afraid? Do I have a confirmed reason to be afraid?" Usually the answer is no. We are people of faith, so first-time meetings are the perfect time to place our fear in the hands of the Lord. We will pray something simple: "Lord, You know us, You know our child, and You know the child's birth family. Please calm the fears of all who are in this meeting. Please allow us to see to the heart of our child's birth family and allow them to see our true heart as well. Amen."

4. Communicate clearly. First introduce yourself and offer a handshake, hug, or smile. Meet your child's birth family the same way you would meet a new neighbor. Don't assume they know who you are. For example, "Hello, I'm Kristin—I'm Sally's foster mom." It sounds so simple, but it is so important. Taking the first step toward introduction will set the tone for future communication. Remember to think of how they are feeling during this meeting. When you choose to reach out first, you are showing that there is nothing to fear, that you are open and welcoming.

5. Find something common between the child and the birth parent. "Wow, he smiles just like you." Think of the connection you would like to have if you were in their shoes. Our daughter sings beautifully, like her biological sister. Our other daughter smiles like her birth mom. Our son laughs like his biological grandmother. Our children need this connection, and so do their first family members. We are not afraid of connection—we celebrate it. Our children's birth parents need to know they are a part of that celebration. We recognize the good that they have passed on to this child.

6. Be confident in your role. You don't need to feel threatened here. It is so easy to feel like we are in competition with a birth parent. We are not in competition. We know who we are, and we stand strong in this role. For adoptive parents, we are the forever family. We get up at all hours of the night to clean up vomit. We are the recipients of hugs, snuggles, and smiles. We don't need to prove our role—we know our role. This is not the time to compete.

7. Allow the birth family member to be the expert. They know what it was like to be pregnant with this child. They know if the child looks like Great-Aunt Freda. There is nothing to fear, so honor the birth parent's role. If the situation makes it difficult to find something positive, find the positive anyway. One of our children's birth mothers ate a ton of spicy food when she was pregnant—every time we talk, we laugh about that child's love of hot sauce.

8. *Ask questions and be interested.* This is just good advice for friendship. Everything you learn can be passed on to your child. The more you learn about the birth family's favorite foods, colors, and hobbies, the more you leave the door open to learn about the story behind the family that created this child that you both love.

24: How can we maintain an open relationship if our child's birth parents are rarely available?

KRISTIN | We adopted our first daughter through a private agency. Her birth mom chose us. She liked that we were a two-parent family with a dog. She liked that we were a family of faith and that we love coffee. She saw something in the pictures and profile that helped her picture her daughter living in our home. She told the agency she could see we would love her daughter.

She also told the agency she wanted her little girl to have a fresh start and a clean slate. She felt it would be too difficult to maintain contact. We felt disappointed but agreed to share pictures and letters through the agency. For years we sent letters and pictures, but as time went on, the relationship really didn't feel like enough.

Mike and I could see our daughter longed to know her first family. She wanted to see her own face reflected in the features of another. We struggled with how to provide something so necessary and natural for our daughter when we didn't have access to it ourselves. Our daughter seemed to sink under the weight of not knowing. Her own inner dialogue began to tell her she was not worthy of knowing, that somehow she was the thing that prevented the relationship. It was hard to convince her that she had been placed for adoption out of love instead of abandonment.

We talked with a good friend who is an adult adoptee about what to do when an open adoption just isn't possible. She encouraged us to

provide openness in adoption regardless of the situation. Openness...
I rolled that word around in my mind for a while. I liked it. Openness
means a willingness, desire, and commitment to share any information
or connection with the child. It means putting the child at the center
of everything and remembering that the most important person in the
relationship between adoptive parents, biological parents, and adoptees is the adoptee. Openness starts with the adoptive parent. We set
the tone for the relationship, and we are often the keepers of information both difficult and good.

So how do we maintain openness when a completely open adoption isn't possible?

1. Honesty. When our child asks a question, we must answer with
honesty. It is our obligation to tell the truth to the best of our ability.
Keeping information from your child will not protect them—it will
build distrust in your relationship. Do your best to allow your child to
hold their own story. Some things are too heavy a burden for a child to
carry at this moment. In that event, tell your child as much as you can.
Let them know that you will tell them more in the future. Set a time to
return to the subject and then keep your promise.

2. Privacy. This is your child's story, not yours. Don't tell anyone
but your child the details—even the simple things like a birth mother's first name. It may be tempting to tell the world that you are adopting and that the child's birth mother loves the color blue. Remember
that the hard parts and the beautiful parts of this story belong to your
child alone.

3. Transparency. Create a transparent relationship with your child.
Do not hide things from him or her. Invite your child to ask the hard
questions just as you would invite your child to ask the fun questions.
Even the tiny details are important. Gather them up like treasures.
Write down things you learn from a former foster parent or professional
who worked with your child. Write down things that your child liked
or a fun conversation you had with a biological family member. Share
these positive things with your child over and over. They are a link to
their past and will become a part of how they create their own identity.

4. Gentleness. Sometimes the things we have to open up to our child about are really difficult. Be gentle with your child and with yourself as you share the tough things. Allow for plenty of time to tell the hard things and allow you child plenty of time—days, weeks, or months— to process the things they have learned. Check in with them often to see if they have any questions or thoughts they would like to share.

25: How can we include the birth family in a natural way?

KRISTIN | Picnics, Thanksgiving dinners, birthday parties, and family reunions are just a few of the simple things I thought I would experience with our family. That was before our family included six sets of birth parents, twelve sets of grandparents, and countless aunts, uncles, and cousins. Trying to add the numbers alone makes my head spin. Our family's everyday activities fill the calendar before the year even begins, so adding special time with biological family can feel like a daunting task. Biological family is so important—spending time with them naturally has been worth our time and energy.

Of course, some biological family members cannot be part of our daily life because of safety or circumstances. Connection is vital for our children, but it isn't always connection to the people you might think. A great-aunt may provide the connection to the child's past they need. A cousin may be a wonderful playmate. Be open to the relationships that are healthy for your child.

1. *Embrace the blending process.* Adoptive families are a type of blended family. One family formed from multiple families. I love the word "blending" because it reminds me of blending colors. Red and blue blended together make purple, blue and yellow make green, and so on. These fresh colors wouldn't exist without first blending two different colors. The vibrant hues of our families wouldn't exist without first blending.

2. *Put yourself in their shoes.* This is the simplest and yet most difficult practice in relationships. How does Grandma feel that her only

grandson is in foster care? How does Aunt Susie feel when she is invited to her nephew's birthday party? Are extended family members feeling sad, angry, hopeless, relieved? Now ask yourself, "If I were feeling this way, what would I want someone to do or say?" I know I would want to hear that the child is safe, loved, and provided for. I would want to know that the child knows about me and our family.

3. *Push past the awkward.* It's going to be awkward. Do you remember hanging out with a friend for the first time? Going on a first date? Meeting your in-laws? Getting to know your child's biological family may be awkward. It's okay if you don't click right away—push through that feeling and pursue common ground wherever you can. Your child will benefit.

4. *Extend opportunities for connection.* You must take initiative here. Invite your child's birth family to join you at a park for an hour. Invite them to meet you at a restaurant for lunch. As your relationship grows, you may want to invite them to do other, more intimate family activities. Some of our children's birth family members invite us for Thanksgiving every year, and we love it! Think of ways you would like to be involved if you were in their shoes. They may be a wonderful addition to the audience at the child's third-grade play. Remember that the ball is in your court. You have the child 24 hours a day, 365 days a year. Take the initiative to extend the welcome first.

5. *Take your child's lead.* Your child may want more or less connection with birth family depending on how they are feeling about the relationship. It is your job as a parent to listen to your child and look for clues to how they are feeling. Sometimes our family gets busy and we haven't seen a family member for a long time, and then one of my kids will ask, "I wonder how Auntie is doing—can we call her?" Take your child's lead here. If your child expresses sadness, anger, or acting out behaviors after a phone call or visit, initiate a conversation with your child and take their cue about when to back off from a relationship for a while.

Ask yourself these questions about interacting with the birth family:

- Who would you welcome into your family if you could?

- Who would you like to build a stronger relationship with?
- Where do you need to set stronger boundaries?
- Where do you need to take the initiative with a family member and invite them in?

26: What if our child idealizes his or her birth family?

KRISTIN | When I was a child, my parents were constantly saying either "Kristin, there is a chair with your name on it" or "Kristin, go sit on your bed." I loved pushing the boundaries. I refused to stop the back talk. I wanted to splash in just one more mud puddle. I was certain that throwing myself on the floor would change the outcome of my current situation. Believe me, Bob and Jenifer Schultz were not messing around. Consistency was not a parenting value they struggled with! They were loving, fair, kind, patient, disciplined, and structured.

During those many trips to my room, I would sit on my bed and lament my family situation. I would press my face to the window and watch the neighborhood kids riding bikes and playing. Their laughter seemed directed toward me, and my anger grew. I would curl up with my abundant assortment of stuffed animals, burrow into the soft, warm pillows, and feel scorned and unfairly punished. Laying there, I could smell a delicious dinner cooking, and even as my mouth watered, I would tell myself that I had the very worst family on the planet. Just as I launched into a daydream about being switched at birth and truly belonging to modern-day royalty (from Ohio), my mom would call me down to dinner. She met me at the bottom of the stairs and talked calmly to me, I apologized, and she hugged me. I never felt shame, only loving and firm direction.

I tell this story because I have a great family. They raised me well. I always felt safe and never had any unmet need. Even so, I dreamed of another family. After asking around, I found that daydreaming about having a mystery family is common. Most children fantasize at some point that they have a long-lost wealthy relative. Or that they have a twin they never knew about. Or that they were adopted and no one ever told them. Despite the fact that I look exactly like my mom, I was convinced as a child that I was adopted and they were just keeping a secret from me.

For our children, all of whom are adopted, this fantasy is much more tangible. They actually do have another family somewhere that they don't live with. A child may know very little about this other family, or they may even see them regularly. Either way, as children's minds grow, they fill in the blanks of their story with things that seem possible. A birth mother who lives in another state becomes a beautiful princess trapped in a tower. A biological parent who is incarcerated becomes a wrongfully accused hero. A parent who has died becomes a misidentified body. Children's imaginations are fantastic and powerful. Sometimes the scenarios are harmless, but sometimes the fantasy can cause damage.

As foster or adoptive parents, it is critical that we check in with our children often about the narrative they have going on inside their minds. Please note that the narrative is different from the feelings they are having. For instance, a child may be feeling sad about his or her adoption. That emotion makes sense because they are disconnected from their first family. However, the child's sadness may come from a narrative they have created about the situation. If the child says, "I'm feeling sad because it's my fault my birth mom was using drugs. I should have tried harder to help her," we now have insight into the story our child is telling in his or her own mind. We know that the child's narrative is not an accurate representation of the situation, and we can better address the emotions surrounding the situation, which are valid.

We talked with a group of adoptees and adoptive parents to gain some insight. We found that the number one thing adoptees want is truth and transparency. We also discovered that adoptive parents struggle most with transparency when they feel the truth may hurt the child.

Our nine-year-old son talks a lot about his adoption narrative, and we have chosen to follow his lead. A few years ago, we were trying to soften the blow while answering a particularly difficult question. He looked us right in the eye and, with wisdom well beyond his years, said,

"Tell me the truth—all of it. I can handle it." So now we do. We always tell the truth when he asks a question. We are always open to discuss and to listen. Some details may be too heavy a burden for our children to carry, but the truth is always best.

Sometimes our children fantasize about their birth family or idealize it. The fantasy may seem harmless, but it is still always best to speak the truth.

How do we support our children as they fill in the gaps of their own story? How do we respond when we realize that our child is filling in the blanks of their own story with things that are not true? Here are a few ideas:

- Always tell the truth, even when it's hard.

- Validate your child's emotions and separate the emotion from the narrative they may be telling themselves.

- Listen to their inner narrative without interruption.

- Correct but do not shame. For instance, if your child says, "My birth mom is a millionaire, and she's going to buy me a new car when I meet her," you may respond by saying, "Wow, that would be really cool. That's a fun thing to think about. I met your birth mom once—do you have any questions about her?"

- Gather as much accurate information as you can about your child's birth family. Even a small detail can help your child build a feeling of connection that is rooted in reality.

- Maintain a connection with your child's birth family if possible. If you know the birth parent or a relative, sometimes a quick phone call can clear up any misconception the child may have.

- Remember, idealizing another person isn't all bad. We all love certain celebrities and maybe even fantasize about what it would be like to meet them or even be friends with them. Celebrities rarely live up to our expectations, and that's okay. It's still important to root ourselves in reality and build solid relationships with those who are in our everyday life.

- The child's fantasy about their birth family does not exist because of you. This simply isn't about the adoptive parent. It's about the child and the child's search for identity.

- Support your child no matter what. When helping them fill in the blanks to their story, remember to never bad-mouth or shame their family members. Remove your emotion from the situation and allow your child to process the good and hard parts of their own story in their own way and in their own time.

27: How do we maintain a connection with the birth family even when it's difficult?

KRISTIN | Of our eight children, we have every type of open adoption possible. We have birth parents who have not been in contact for years and birth family who call or stop by randomly just to say hello. Maintaining contact with healthy and safe birth family is obviously the easiest relationship to navigate. But in our years as foster and adoptive parents, we have held relationships with birth families who were in jail, out of the country, or just not emotionally healthy for the child. We have experienced the death and therefore permanent loss of connection with a birth family member. How can we stay connected with a birth family when it is difficult or impossible to do so?

You must maintain a connection with your child's birth family to the best of your ability. We cannot force connection where there is none. The tricky part of foster and adoption is finding a healthy balance for our children. We believe that openness in adoption is always best. Openness in adoption means we are transparent with our children. We support them as they navigate a relationship with their first family. Sometimes we can't have contact, or sometimes we simply don't have or know the information our children want or need.

Here are a few guidelines to follow:

1. *Determine the relationship.* What does the relationship look like, and what would you like it to look like? What type of contact will benefit the child? What does the child want from the relationship and is this possible? What does the birth parent want and is this possible? Advocate for your child to have the healthiest relationship possible.

2. *Set a boundary.* Adoptions consist of all types of connectedness. You and your child may want to write letters or emails to the birth family or share pictures monthly. If you need some distance, set up a post office box or communicate through email. If you feel comfortable sharing openly, get connected on social media. Setting a boundary means deciding what you and your child are comfortable with and what is healthy for the child. Boundaries may change over time. Keeping communication open can prevent miscommunication and hurt feelings for you, your child, and your child's first family.

3. *Maintain connection to the best of your ability.* It is possible that an ongoing connection with a birth family is not possible. If a child's birth parent has passed away or lives out of the country or is unnamed, this can leave the child feeing an emptiness about his or her own past. It is important that we do our best to keep a connection for the child in any way possible.

Incorporating the child's culture of origin into our everyday lives is one way we can stay connected. Holding on to pieces of information for the child, such as the birth parent's favorite color, a photograph, or a story you know about the parent, can help the child feel connected to his or her own past.

4. *Keep an open dialogue with your child.* We don't know what we don't know. Staying in communication with our child first is essential to maintaining a healthy connection to birth family. Your child may be longing to know something about his or her birth family but unable to formulate the words to tell you. Your child may be feeling like he or she needs a break from their birth family for a while. Once you know what the child is feeling, your job is to support them. You may need to hunt

down answers for your child, or you may need to redefine a boundary the child has become uncomfortable with. We always try to teach our children to advocate for themselves, and the first way they learn that is by practicing with us. When they set a boundary of their own or share a desire with us, our job is to support them.

5. *Prioritize what's best for the child.* Adoptees are the center of adoption. Their needs, wants, desires, security, identity, and safety are our top priority—always. As we navigate ongoing relationships with a birth family, we must always ask ourselves, How will this affect the child? The answer to this question will determine our path.

28: How can we support our child when the birth parents terminate their parental rights?

KRISTIN | When our son came to live with us, it was only supposed to be for the weekend. Nine years later, he's still here! We fell in love with him when he was just three days old. His journey through foster care was a roller coaster of emotions. We planned to say goodbye to him multiple times, only to leave court with one more failed attempt at reunification. The day we walked into his final team meeting at the Department of Child Services, we had no idea what was about to happen.

His mom was facing termination of her parental rights after 18 months in the system. We had grown to love her and planned to partner with her for as long as it would take to get her child back and raise him well. The move toward termination was a relief for us as well as a great sadness. The caseworker started the meeting and then turned to the mom for her to speak.

She turned to look at me and asked, "Will you please adopt him? I know I'm not going to get him back, and I want to be a part of planning for him to have a family."

I was shocked, relieved, sad, and overjoyed. My mouth dropped open. Our son was too young to understand what was happening at the time, but over the years, he has had to process what happened second-hand through stories and answered questions.

Our older children were old enough to understand the termination as it was happening. As the second-choice parents, we had to figure out how to support our children through their myriad of emotions. If your foster child's case is moving toward termination, here are some things to remember as you offer support:

1. Foster parenting is temporary; adoption is forever. When we foster, we spend weeks, months, and even years as the temporary parents. We assure our children that they are going to go home. If they aren't moving toward home, we assure them that their parents love them and are working toward becoming healthy. As things change in the case, we may comfort the child during missed visits, difficult court hearings, and frustrating team meetings.

When termination happens, we have to shift our thinking and behavior from temporary family to forever family. This shift takes time, often years or decades. This is okay. It's important to acknowledge the shift.

2. Transition to adoption is often difficult. Our children have been thinking temporarily, but now this family is forever. We can support our children by talking about the transition. We need to allow our child to take as much time as necessary to trust that we are not going to leave. Be patient.

3. Recognize that children may feel divided loyalty. A child may be excited about the adoption one day and angry about it the next. They may feel disconnected from their birth family one day and longing for connection the next. We can support them through this by listening, talking, and never saying bad things about their birth family. Children need to know it's okay to love both families.

4. Find a counselor who will support the child and the whole family. Seek a counselor who understands trauma, adoption, and attachment. When you find a good counselor, this can be a safe place for the child to unload fear, resentment, misunderstandings about their journey, and more. If the counselor you choose is working toward bonding with the family, she or he will pull you into the sessions as well and help form the new attachment.

5. Utilize post-adoption services. Some states and agencies offer post-adoption services. They may offer classes, home-based counseling, parent coaching, and respite. Do some research and find professional supports for yourself and your child.

6. Initiate conversation. Your child may not want to talk about all that is happening. They may feel abandoned or ashamed by all that has transpired. Start the conversation. Let your child know that this subject is never off-limits and that any emotion they are feeling is valid. Listen and be a safe place for your child to share when they feel ready.

7. Uphold a positive, peaceful relationship with first family to the best of your ability. Do your very best to be kind in your language and interactions with the birth family. It is important for your child to see that you value the place they have come from. Find the good and acknowledge the hard things. Children need to see that you are confident in who you are and that you are strong enough to keep the peace.

29: How can I support the first parents when they lose their parental rights?

KRISTIN | Sometimes children cannot return to their first parents but cannot stay in the limbo of foster care. A different solution must be found. If no other suitable family member is found, the child may be adopted by the foster parents. We rejoiced when our children were able to stay, but the joy is always tempered by the deep loss that our children and their parents are experiencing. We cannot always be a part of the birth family's support system, but often we are. How do we move from supporting the parents in reunification to supporting the parents through their loss?

Here are seven guidelines to keep in mind as you support your child's birth parents:

1. Remember that foster parenting is temporary. Foster care is designed to provide a place for children to be safe until the biological family is capable of providing a stable environment. Our job as foster parents includes cheering on the biological parents, comforting the child, and advocating for the best interest of the child no matter what.

2. Build peaceful relationships to the best of your ability. If it is possible, build healthy relationships with everyone in your child's community. Begin this process before you reach termination, before the question of adoption arises. Do your best to get to know your child's family. You are giving a gift to another human when you extend friendship.

We often found that by simply complimenting the birth family on their beautiful, smart, talented child, we offer just the words that are needed to let the family know we are fostering as a part of their support group, not against them. Ask the family questions about the child and about themselves. When we were foster parents, we found ourselves in countless hours of courtroom waiting rooms—sitting on hard plastic chairs, reading outdated magazines, waiting anxiously. These are the times we were able to reach out to our children's birth families.

Getting to know them helped us support them well. Getting to know them helped our children see that we value their family and their history. Sometimes we can't see our children's birth family after the adoption—in those cases, our children cling to the stories we share, those small pieces of their identity.

3. Initiate conversation. You have the upper hand, so reach out first. Reach out to biological parents throughout the foster care journey. Ask them questions about themselves. Offer positive information about the children. Invite them to celebrate successes and allow them to be a part of the solution if things are difficult.

I found out from a birth mom of one of our children that an allergy to dairy runs in the family. I would have found out eventually, but because we were talking with one another, I was able to find the solution to the toddler's fussy behavior and skin irritation much more quickly.

It is vital to find common ground with your child's other parents, especially when they lose their parental rights. It's okay to grieve with your child's first parents. It's okay to be disappointed with them. It's okay to feel conflicted with the emotions of relief, sadness, anger, and love.

4. Show compassion. Everyone receives love differently. It may not always be appropriate to hug a birth parent or write a letter or cry with them. If you have been building a relationship all along, you will know in your gut what to do. Be silent when you need to and reach out when you need to. Sometimes I feel anger toward our child's birth parents for hurting the child. That emotion is okay too. Always do your best to show compassion and grace.

5. *Show respect.* This is hard when a person has hurt a child we love. By the time a parent has lost rights to be the parent, even when you are fed up or angry, show respect. Your child is watching. Your child was created by that person you are angry with. Be kind in your words. Do not bash your child's family. It's okay to say, "I'm angry about what happened to you." Be honest, truthful, and always respectful.

6. *Set boundaries where needed.* As the case moves toward termination, some parents will grasp for ways to get their child back or be involved after the adoption. Set boundaries when needed. Be clear with expectations. Creating a post-adoption agreement will help both sets of parents know what to expect.

7. *Keep your child's best interests in mind.* At the center of all of this is the child. The adoption has been determined to be in their best interest. That doesn't mean they aren't struggling. They need to see you support their first family. They need to hear your language of grace, compassion, and respect. Your child needs you to put him or her first throughout this whole process.

30: What if safety is a concern?

MIKE | Sometimes members of a birth family are not safe, and there is reason to take extra precautions and measures.

Several years ago, we were connected to a family who had adopted a sibling group in Minnesota. From all accounts, everything was cordial and peaceful between the adoptive parents and the birth parents. In fact, it wasn't out of the ordinary for the birth parents and the adoptive parents to get together with the children regularly.

However, concerns began arising after several months of permanency—not with the birth parents, but with the birth parents' extended family members. The aunt of the birth father began following our friends and their precious children—at their school playground, at the grocery store, at their church, even in the mall and local park near their home. Late at night, after the kids were in bed, our friends sometimes saw the aunt sitting in a minivan in front of their house staring at them. A few times, the aunt tried to pick the kids up after school, claiming she was asked by our friends to do so.

Finally, the adoptive parents called the police.

The aunt had a criminal record and was not considered by authorities to be a safe or stable person. Our friends were on high alert all the time! It was exhausting, frustrating, and terrifying. After giving the woman many warnings, the police eventually had no option but to place a restraining order on her.

You may have similar stories. As safe and peaceful as the adoption and foster care process usually is, there can be a measure of danger depending on the stability of the birth parents and their family. Never let fear control you and dictate how you behave and interact with others. When there is a legitimate concern, take measures to ensure the safety of your family.

Whether you're just beginning the journey or you are seasoned at being a foster or adoptive parent, here are some steps to take if you find yourself in an unsafe situation:

1. Make sure all vital parties are informed. The instant there is a legitimate safety concern, make sure you notify everyone who has contact with your child. Call for a brief emergency meeting at your child's school. Meet with the principal, the bus driver, and the people working at the front office. If your child plays sports, notify the coach. Meet with his or her small-group leader or youth pastor at church to make sure they are aware of the situation.

2. Print the person's picture. Find a color picture that can be printed clearly. Many years ago, when we were still working for a church, we had some big concerns over the family of a child we were fostering. We scoured the internet for the best pictures we could find, printed them, and called a meeting with the entire youth and children's ministry staff at the church to discuss the situation. Every person who had contact with the child received a picture of the people we were concerned about.

3. Create a safety plan everyone agrees on. Our three-step safety plan looks something like this: (1) Determine a simple safety response if an unsafe person is near the child. Make sure the child is with a trusted adult in a secure area. (2) Notify a parent as soon as possible. (3) Notify a police officer.

Keep a written plan and distribute it to those who need to know.

4. Inform your child... if he or she is at an appropriate age. We believe children eight years or older should be informed of the situation. Keep your language simple and calm.

In his book *The Gift of Fear*, Gavin DeBecker explains that we are all wired with an intuition to know when something is unsafe or volatile. Unfortunately, we are the only species on earth that doesn't listen to that intuition out of fear of being rude or hurtful to someone. When a situation is unsafe, we need to sound an alarm.

31: What if the birth family cannot connect in a healthy way?

KRISTIN | We believe that connection with a child's first family and family history is vital. Not all family members are safe, but some type of connection should be maintained if possible. As our children are heading into adulthood, they may be interested in connecting with family members who have previously not been part of their lives. When this family member is known to be in an unhealthy or dangerous place, this can be terrifying. What can we do to support our children when they are exercising their right to their own history and their own family?

1. Be honest. If we know something, it is our duty to be honest with our child. Never hide the details from your child. They will find out eventually, and they will lose trust in you if you kept it from them. When the child is young, we share details in an age-appropriate way. As a child grows, they need to know more details. If the child pushes forward with contact, be honest with your child about your concerns while also being supportive. Initiate the conversation with your child and be open to any questions or conversation they want to have.

2. Set boundaries. Some children may be able to build a healthy relationship with birth family that involves visiting, meeting up somewhere, or inviting them to school events. (Some children will not be able to have this type of relationship.) If this is the case, allow your child to navigate the new relationship with some firm boundaries in place. You may meet up at a restaurant to talk and allow the child some semiprivate time to talk while you sit at another table and read a book. You will know your own situation and what boundaries need to be in place.

3. Provide a safe space. Your child may feel every emotion possible over this relationship. They need a soft place to land, and it needs to be you. Remember to never criticize your child's birth family. Experience joy with your child. Feel the sadness with them too. Let your child know you are strong enough to walk with them through any emotion.

4. Connect with adult adoptees. Help your child get connected with adult adoptees. They will have the personal experience to share with your child, and they can become trusted people to share emotions with throughout the entire process, even when it's a roller coaster.

5. Step in if necessary. Some relationships simply aren't healthy. We desire for our children to be connected to birth family in some way. Sometimes they will experience hurt or rejection from birth family. Step in if things are getting out of hand. Let your child know that you love them more than anything and you will do anything to keep them safe and healthy. They are your number one priority, and they should hear you say that, especially if the reunion is disappointing or unhealthy.

32: What if my adult child stops communicating with me?

KRISTIN | Your 25-year-old daughter hasn't answered a call in four weeks and didn't show up to Christmas dinner. Your 21-year-old son seems angry and distant every time you are together. Your 18-year-old daughter just left for college, and even though your goodbye was sweet and genuine, she is disappointed in you all the time and won't tell you why. Your adult son just got married and is enthralled with his wife's family but doesn't want anything to do with his family. What can we do when our adult child stops communicating?

1. Understand. Rejection hurts, even from a child or, in this case, an adult child. Seek to understand your child's perspective first. Trauma will always be a part of your child's story. It does not have to define them, but it can change their perspective on relationships throughout life, including their relationship with you. Is there a life change that may have triggered the emotional distance? Did you have a falling out? Is there a pattern to their disappearance, such as a certain time of year or event that happens around the time they retreat?

Understand that children who have been adopted may always carry a fear of rejection, loss, or unworthiness. An adoptee may see their own failures magnified through the lens of adoption. They may fear doing better or worse than their birth family. They may fear being more successful or less successful than their adoptive parents. Life changes can cause a return of the feelings surrounding the previous trauma. The birth of a child reminds them they were separated from their first mom. A marriage reminds them they didn't know their first father. The trigger can be anything, but when the reaction is to put walls up and run from family, it can be confusing for those who love the adult child.

2. Invite but keep expectations low. Invite your child to be a part of things the family is doing but keep the invitation light. Communicate clearly over text message, email, or voicemail even if they don't answer. Do not shame if they don't return your call or show up. Remind them consistently that you will be available whenever they are ready to talk again and that you love spending time with them. Invite them to dinner but don't set out the extra plate until they arrive. Place their Christmas presents in a separate pile and put them under the tree when they pull into the driveway. Keep your grandchildren's presents in a special place and celebrate with them whenever you get to see them. Make a point to enjoy the moments together even if they may not happen again for a long time.

3. Don't stop living. Don't postpone family pictures for four years, hoping to have the family all together. Don't cancel your birthday party because you fear one person may not come. Enjoy the family that is present. Enjoy your life. Pursue the child but do not let that pursuit stop you from living. When the child returns your call or stops by on Christmas Day, it will be an added joyous occasion!

33: How can we initiate a conversation with our child's school about trauma?

KRISTIN | We respect our children's school and appreciate their professionalism in all areas of teaching. However, the effects of trauma are widely misunderstood. Many professionals don't know the signs of trauma, the prevalence of childhood trauma, and the tools to use with students.

When our son was eight years old, he hit a teacher. Mike and I sat in the conference room with the principal, the teacher, the special education teacher, and the guidance counselor. As the story unfolded, we realized that the conflict began with an iPad. Our son had iPad time near the end of the school day. The teacher warned him that his time was up and then grabbed the device from his hand. Our son panicked at the touch and spun around quickly to punch her. He felt ashamed at his reaction, and she felt angry and surprised. We suddenly realized that our son's experience with domestic violence played a role in our child's reaction. We took the opportunity to explain what happened to his team. They were very supportive, but we knew we should have approached them earlier. Here is what we would do differently:

1. Gather materials. Copy some of the most important and easily understandable material you have about trauma. Keep this simple. You do not want to overwhelm the school with information. They have to learn a little bit about a lot of children! This information should be basic and easy to read. Print a page of tools you find effective at home with your child or any language you use with your child that you need them to support you with. For instance, we use the term "safe people" for people our children can talk to about the trauma. Our teachers also know the safe people so they can redirect our children if they are sharing something private with students or staff who do not need to know the details.

2. Reach out to the teacher, principal, and counselor. They will set the tone for the school and ultimately your child's school experience. First, set up a phone chat. If more information is needed, set up a time to talk face-to-face with the staff who need to know some important parts of the child's history. This small group of people can become your child's support team.

3. Offer a short training during a staff meeting or an individualized education program (IEP) meeting. If you or someone you know (such as a counselor, pediatrician, or post-adoption worker) is comfortable, offer a small training on childhood trauma at the next staff meeting. This can be a 15-minute lesson on how trauma changes the brain and a few handy tools to use with children who are triggered by past trauma.

4. Share resources and tools. When you read something new, share it with the school. Copy small parts of an article, share a new coping skill your child learned, or even invite someone from your child's school to attend a conference or training in your area about trauma.

34: How can we identify people who are not helpful?

KRISTIN | Foster care and adoption can often be very lonely. Most people don't understand our families and therefore keep their distance. Few venture out to find out more about our way of living. Among those few are people who are genuinely interested in being a part of the support system as well as people who are not interested in supporting our families in a healthy way. It is important to identify those who offer genuine support and those who do not. Here are a few red flags to look out for:

1. Someone who is nosey. "So what did the mother do?" She drew out the "o" in *do* like it was an entirely separate word. The woman stopped by with a casserole and a jug of milk. I was grateful for the food, but the questions were unnerving. We had a new placement in our foster home. A teenage girl. We weren't accustomed to people bringing meals to our house for a foster placement, and it was a breath of fresh air. I welcomed her warmly, but her question cut the pretense like a knife.

My jaw dropped, and I looked quickly behind me to make sure my foster daughter wasn't within earshot. She was. I saw her shoulders stiffen, and I fumbled for the words that would show appreciation for the dinner while expressing that our daughter's mother was not up for discussion.

"Thank you so much for dinner! I don't want to keep you another minute," I replied, and walked briskly back to the door. Nearly shoving her out, I said goodbye. I locked the door and returned to try to mend things with our daughter. People who just want to get the scoop on our family are not the people we want around us. It's okay to decline help from these people.

2. Someone who isn't willing to follow your parenting style. Our daughter sat in time-out with her lower lip protruding and one single tear dripping from her saddened eyes. She had done something quite deserving of a time-out and was taking a few minutes to chill out in my office just off the church lobby. It was a Sunday morning, and I had my hands full with people and tasks. Suddenly I looked around the corner to find a woman kneeling next to our daughter offering her a lollipop.

The woman was not trying to disrespect our parenting, but she was clearly undoing the reset time our daughter needed in that moment. She was misreading the situation and damaging our bond with our child by offering her a sucker. I know this is difficult for others to understand, but foster and adoptive families must balance discipline with bonding.

I walked briskly across the lobby and politely asked the woman not to give her a treat: "Thank you for checking on her. I know she appreciates it. She just has a few more minutes on her time-out, and then I bet she'd love to come find you to say good morning." I smiled, and the woman apologized. Our daughter was able to finish her calm-down time and then visit with that woman later. There was even a lollipop still there for her.

3. Someone who opposes your value system. We are in a careful dance with our children, and we need people around us who understand our children's struggles and strengths. Someone who purposely tries to do something against our value system should be asked to stop.

In our family, we do not buy a car for a child. If someone offers to buy a car for our child, we will politely decline the offer. If someone persists, we will ask the person to stop. If they insist, we will ask them to leave. A car is an extreme example, but many of us have dealt with people offering to help in a way that doesn't fit with our boundaries or values as a family. Our values exist for a reason. They are the things we agree on as a family that are a part of what makes up the character of who we are. A good friend and support system will abide by those values with our children.

4. Someone who wants to be the hero. Who doesn't want to be the hero? I do. But I'm not. Our child is the hero of this story. The neighbor who is trying to get my kids out of time-out is not the hero. The grandma who is giving my kids a food that agitates them is not the hero. The auntie who wants to keep the kids up well past bedtime, disregarding our schedule, is not the hero.

5. Someone who doesn't look out for our best interests. You may meet someone who thinks they would have been a better parent for your child. Often people feel entitled to adoptive and foster children as if they are somehow community property. They are not. If someone doesn't cheer your family on, if someone implies they could do a better job, it is probably time to stop interacting with that person.

Some people *can* do some things with our children better than we can. I am terrible at math, so our child will need a math tutor to help him. That person will be better at math than me, and that's okay. But that person will not start being our child's mother. They are there to support me as a mom and support our child as a student by helping him with math.

Other people may be good encouragers or good friends or wise mentors. These are all good things, but they are still not the mom. They are a part of the support system. Someone who insists on crossing this boundary isn't a healthy part of your support system.

6. *Someone who doesn't recognize your expertise.* Our pediatrician constantly turns to us for information about our children. She says, "You know your child best." She asks thought-provoking questions that get to the bottom of whatever the mystery is that brought us to her in the first place. She is the expert at being the doctor. We are the experts at knowing if our child slept through the night, had a weird poopy diaper, or is having trouble focusing. Someone who doesn't recognize our role as the parents isn't a helpful person to have around. They may miss important facts that would help the child.

7. *Someone who hinders your authority and pushes your boundaries.* "What happens at Grandma's house stays at Grandma's house." The sign in my friend's kitchen was meant to be funny. I understand that. But as I read it over and over, I felt icky. Mike and I have been lucky that our parents don't challenge our authority with our kids, and they never undermine our decisions. But other adoptive and foster parents battle this type of damaging behavior from friends and family members.

These are the people who say "Oh, one little cookie won't hurt—just don't tell Mom!" or "I'd let you stay up later, but you know your dad... we don't want to get in trouble with him!" People who undermine often do it in a joking, passive-aggressive tone, making it uncomfortable to confront. These people are not helping, they are harming. Foster and adoptive families are working hard to build trust through appropriate boundaries and consistency. One "fun aunt" can do incredible damage by crossing even a small boundary.

8. *Someone who gets offended when you don't do things their way.* Just walk away from these people. If they feel they can do it better, they may want to use their energy toward a new hobby or something else. A firm boundary is necessary with people who just want to do things their way. The child you have been entrusted with is precious and worthy of the

structure, love, and lifestyle you are providing. Children who have lost their first families need to know that the mom and dad they have now are going to take good care of them. The friend, neighbor, or relative who demands that you heed their unsolicited advice is taking away from the attention your child actually needs from you.

Part 3

ATTACHMENT PARENTING

35: Why aren't traditional parenting methods working for us?

MIKE | Kristin and I both grew up in traditional households with traditional parenting. These techniques were not bad, they were just… traditional. There were rules and restrictions, guidelines and boundaries. If established rules, restrictions, guidelines, and boundaries were crossed, consequences were enforced. No questions asked.

These techniques appear to have worked. We both grew up to be responsible adults who know the difference between right and wrong. We are completely capable of making wise choices and using coping skills when we're feeling overwhelmed.

Neither of us endured significant trauma as children. And that was the game changer.

When we first became parents, we thought we had a healthy understanding of how to raise kids. In 2004 a little girl and boy came to live with us through foster care and soon became permanent family members.

When the little girl turned seven, I caught her in a straight-up lie. When I asked her why she lied, she just stared at me. I continued to question her…and question her. Her eyes started darting around the room. She wouldn't look at me. She would open her mouth to speak but nothing came out. I'd love to tell you my heart gave way and I stopped. Not the case. I became more frustrated. Finally I'd had enough and marched her off to her room. The night was over for her. In my mind, she was content with her "bad behavior" and needed a stiff consequence—time away from others to "think" about it. For several more years, I parented with this black-and-white thinking.

I was raised this way, and I would parent this way too! However, I was never starving. I never bounced from foster home to foster home. I never witnessed domestic violence. I never grew up in an orphanage or group home. My mom and dad always took care of me, and more important, they were always there for me. Our children were missing this key element. The result was deep cavernous wounds. When I finally realized this, it changed the way I communicated with our children and reacted to their behavior.

I've discovered that traditional parenting, the way I was parented, just doesn't work with our kiddos. Here are just three of the many reasons this is the case:

1. *Trauma changes the brain.* If your child was drug and alcohol exposed in utero, subject to abuse, malnourished, neglected, or in and out of foster homes, their brain has been altered by this trauma. Their perspective and their behavior are changed. They are thinking, behaving, reacting, and surviving out of loss. You cannot look at your child and ask, "What were you thinking?" Chances are, they don't know. If you continue to demand an answer or lecture, you cause your child to shut down.

2. *Their behavior is a voice.* For years I thought our son's choices, reactions, and attitude were because he liked being bad. I disciplined him according to this belief. One night I stood indignantly in my upstairs bathroom while he threw the mother of all tantrums and attempted to tip over a solid-steel claw-foot bathtub. I was furious. I wanted to ground him for life. He was traumatizing our other children and causing me to miss out on my night as well.

Yes, he was behaving badly, but it wasn't because he was a bad kid. His behavior was a voice from his traumatic past. It was an outcry. He was not fighting against me but against an intense situation that he could not process. When I realized his behavior was actually a voice, I started reacting differently.

3. *Fight, flight, or freeze.* These fear responses are how our kiddos respond to intense situations. If you tend to give lectures (like we used to), you've probably noticed it doesn't work. When we lecture, our kids shut down because they are in survival mode.

36: What are some traditional parenting methods to avoid?

MIKE | Once we discover that traditional parenting doesn't work, it's time to take the next step. Now let's look at some specific habits to avoid:

1. Don't shame. It's easy to shift into a shaming mode even if you don't intend to. We often just want a reaction from our children. The problem with shaming is that it reinforces our children's belief that they are failures, not good enough, and unloved.

2. Don't lecture. Shaming and lecturing are valuable tools if your only goal is to get a response. Of course, we want much more than that for our kids. As a kid, when I was on the receiving end of a lecture, I simply resolved to work harder to not get caught. When your child shuts down, your connection with them will be lost.

3. Don't lose your cool. You and I are personally invested in this journey with our kiddos, so our emotions are often wrapped up in it. Your heightened emotion becomes a trigger that causes your child's emotions to heighten.

4. Don't give in. Boundaries are good for our children. Children who have experienced significant trauma have rarely experienced appropriate boundaries. They may push back when you establish boundaries. Remember that a boundary means that you love them. They are strong enough to live within this boundary. If you give in, you will undo the security that the boundary is helping to form.

37: What do kids who have experienced trauma need?

KRISTIN | "If you don't stop holding that baby, she's never going to learn to walk," a nosey middle-aged man exclaimed in the church lobby for all to hear. My ten-month-old daughter, already an introvert by nature, was wrapped around my body like a koala. For her, the church lobby was a place to be endured. She hated the bustle, the noise, and the constant attention. As a pastor's family and a transracial adoptive family, we were often the center of attention.

Most people in our community just loved our daughter, and her presence brought joy to them. A handful of people felt obliged to share their parenting advice every time we turned a corner. At ten months old, our daughter wasn't walking, it's true. It's also not outside the norm for typical development. I would have held any of my babies in that crazy after-church mob, but the choice to hold this child was intentional. She needed more. I knew it to my core—she didn't just *want* to be held, she *needed* to be held. This child needed the slow steps toward security that would eventually lead her to independence.

By the way, the man in the lobby was wrong. I kept holding her, and one day she stretched her long legs and took off on her own two feet.

When our children have lost something as vital to their very being as a mom and dad, they need specific parenting strategies to heal from the trauma. They don't just want more than other kids, and they aren't manipulating for more time, more space, more attention, more patience. Here are some things they *need*:

1. *Time together.* Children learn about trust and security in the months before they are born and the months after. If neglect, abuse, or separation has happened during this time, it will leave lasting insecurity. Parents who wish to create healthy attachments will have to spend extra time building trust. Our kids may need us to sit with them while they fall asleep. They may need us to eat lunch with them during their school day, even in high school. They may need us to volunteer to chaperone on a field trip or just stop by the school to drop off a lunch box. They need us to intentionally set aside time to be completely dialed in to their lives.

2. *Patience.* Our kids need extra patience. They have experienced something that we were not a part of and that most of us did not experience firsthand. Our children will work through their trauma in different ways at different times. If your child is behaving poorly, there may be a deeper reason for what's going on. They may not be able to identify what has caused the behavior or their reaction to the trigger. We

need to show extra patience. We may appear to be allowing inappropriate behavior, but that is not the case.

One of our sons could not attend the worship time during church. He screamed and covered his ears, his body writhing on the floor. It was embarrassing and frustrating. We left church each Sunday in a bustle of humiliation. Then we realized that he is extra sensitive to light and sound. We got him a pair of headphones to wear during church, and we chose not to enter the worship area until the music portion was done. Some people thought we were babying him. Exactly the opposite is true. Once we were patient enough to get past the tantrum, we were able to see that the behavior was about his discomfort. By helping him find the tools to succeed, he was able to attend church and other places like the movie theater and a hockey game. He wasn't being a brat—he was expressing a need. Being patient enough to get to the bottom of the behavior wasn't enabling him, it was empowering him. By empowering him to express his feelings and meet his needs, we built our own attachment with him. His trust grew when he realized that we were there to help, not harm.

3. Guidance. We give our children a gift when we teach them to say "I feel." Our children need an outlet to work through their trauma. As they grow in their attachment to us, they can heal from past hurts. Our children will need attachment, trust, and security as they grow into adults. Because these things were disrupted, we will have to go back and reteach what should have come naturally.

Teaching kids how to feel is vital to building attachment. When a child is a newborn, parents meet their every need. Through trial and error, parents learn to understand the child's language. When a child is adopted at an older age, Mom and Dad are not in sync with that early unspoken language. Parents must guide their children toward mutually understood language.

4. Only a few caregivers. No, you may not hold my baby. I'm aware that everyone wants to hold the baby. I want to hold all the babies too, but when a family is working on building attachment, all interactions with others must be intentional. Build a close support system around you but remember that not every person is a part of that system.

A front carrier is useful for keeping extra hands off infants. We found that having our infants close to us built our attachment and prevented extra attention, which our children didn't need at that time. Older children could hold a hand, ride in a stroller, or go fewer places with you.

Find a babysitter who will understand the importance of consistency in attachment. We know that sometimes sitters, teachers, bus drivers, and friends will change. That's okay, but to the best of our ability, we try to keep our circle small. This is at least as important with foster kids as it is with adopted kids. Foster children already feel that their world may change at any moment, so do your best to keep the world around your family predictable and small.

5. *Modeling.* Talk about trust and attachment with your children. Model healthy attachments with people in your own life. Create healthy relationships around yourself, and be open with your child about your choices: "I'm friends with Miss Nicole and Miss Megan because they are honest, trustworthy, and kind." Modeling healthy attachment allows your child to see the benefit to bonding.

6. *Strengthening, not enabling.* Others may look into our lives from the outside and feel that in our effort to help our children heal, we are actually spoiling them. Our compassion can lead to enabling, so it's important to ask yourself often, "Am I strengthening or enabling our child?"

Our son loves to sleep in our bed. If he could, he would happily stay there all night with one foot in my face and an elbow in my husband's back. This would not be healthy for any of us. We want him to feel safe and secure and independent at bedtime, so there are some steps we have decided to take to help him build that confidence. We allow him to start out in our bed when he's feeling anxious, and then we move him to his bed when it's time for us to sleep. This allows him to feel secure without inadvertently teaching him that he cannot sleep on his own. If he is afraid at night, we are always willing to hug him, pray with him, and tuck him back in. We may sit beside his bed for a little bit, but we don't stay there all night or move him back to our bed. This is intentional. We want our son to know we are always here and will always do our best to keep him safe. We want him to also learn that he is safe in his room. He is brave and strong, and he can stay in his room by himself.

7. *Strengthening through balance.* Strengthening our children is about finding balance. Giving our children the tools to use on their own is not enabling—it is teaching. Our children have coping skills they can use when they are away from us. They can do some things on their own to help with anxiety. They know that we have given them these tools so the time away is not damaging our bond, it is strengthening it.

One of our sons hated going to preschool. I wanted to pull him out and just keep him home, but our counselor at the time helped me see that he was having fun at preschool, but he was just having anxiety about separating. We created a ten-step process: Stay in the classroom, then move to sitting by the door, then move outside the door, then stay in the building, and so on until I was able to leave him all morning and he could trust I was going to come back.

Others thought we were babying him, but they just didn't understand the amount of trauma our child had from feeling abandoned. Our counselor and our son's teachers understood that our son had a valid reason for needing our presence more than other students. They also understood that it was vital for our son to eventually attend school on his own. By working together, we were all able to help him create a new sense of confidence.

8. *Strengthening, not rescuing.* Strengthening our children is not rescuing. When our children are struggling, it is difficult to resist rescuing them from the bad test grade, the difficult friendship, or some legal trouble. Strengthening our children means we stand by their side while they go through the tough thing. We do not rescue, but we do stand strong.

A child who has lost their first family may need more reassurance that we are still here and we still love them. We may say something like, "I know it was embarrassing for you to have to miss recess today for fighting. I know you are strong enough to take the consequence. I want you to know that I love you very much and nothing will ever change that." Our kids don't need to be rescued, but they may need to be reassured.

9. Help distinguishing behavior from emotion. "I know you are feeling…but you may not…" This is a sentence we say often in our home. Outsiders may hear this conversation and make a judgment about what we should do: "Well, I would just wash his mouth out with soap if he ever talked to me that way!" Okay, okay. I know that our child's reaction to things is sometimes over the top. I know that our child's dysregulation is uncomfortable and just looks like a tantrum, but stick with me here. By addressing the reason for our child's behavior, I can help our child cope in a more acceptable way in the future: "I know you are feeling frustrated, but you may not punch. What can we do instead?" When we separate our child's emotion from their behavior, we give them a chance to address the feeling in a way that will be productive, not destructive.

10. Structure, consistency, and follow-through. Why do we always leave the neighborhood cookout at 8:00 on the dot? Because we have to. I parent differently because our child is learning to trust. Our child doesn't do well when things change, and he or she needs to follow the same structure every day. If I maintain consistency, our child can learn to trust, and one day we may be able to stay later at the party. We may be able to skip bath time or go to bed without brushing teeth. But for now, I am teaching the trust through consistency that was disrupted for our child in his or her early life.

11. Yes or no but not maybe. My mom and dad always said maybe. They didn't want to promise something and not follow through. This made sense to me as a child. If I asked for ice cream after dinner, they said, "I don't know…maybe. We'll see if you eat a healthy dinner and finish your chores." This was fun for me. It was always a kind of challenge, a mystery. We didn't often get ice cream, but when we did, it was such a treat. The "maybe" felt like a fun adventure.

For our children, "maybe" isn't an adventure. It brings up feelings of uncertainty. Maybe they will have a forever family. Maybe Mom will show up to the visit tonight. Maybe we will have enough food. In our home, we must answer yes or no. We need to be as certain as we can possibly be with our children as they are building trust. If we don't think ice cream after dinner is a for-sure thing, we will say no first. We may get to go back later and say, "I know we said no to ice cream tonight, but we have a little extra time before bed and you are already done with your chores. What do you think about going out for a special treat tonight?" To the best of our ability, we need to give our children clear answers as we build trust and attachment.

38: How can we find the right therapist for our family?

MIKE | The foster and adoption journeys are not easy. Your children have come from traumatic pasts that will play out in their behaviors, the way they interact with the world, and their connection with you. Trauma can cause secondary trauma to occur among the rest of your family. You and your children will benefit from the support of an effective therapist. The need for professional help is not a sign of failure.

How do you choose the right therapist for your family? There are probably many therapists available for you to choose from. Most would claim to understand the foster and adoptive parenting journey. Many claim to understand kiddos from trauma. But how do you know for sure? We have personally gone through the gauntlet of good therapists, not-so-good therapists, and complete-and-utter-disaster therapists. These are some crucial questions to ask when finding the person who can best serve you and your family:

1. *Are they supportive of you and your family?* You will know this within the first visit or two. If a therapist is not working hard to understand what is happening with you and to support your current efforts, then it's time to say goodbye.

2. *Do they understand and embrace the foster and adoptive journey?* It's one thing to understand something—it's another thing to embrace it. Embracing something means you understand not only the "what" but also the "why" behind it.

3. Do they have a working knowledge of trauma? Do they use this knowledge in their language and actions? A therapist can be informed about trauma and understand it conceptually but have very little working knowledge of it. Many people are informed of the effects of prenatal drug and alcohol exposure but have no idea how that plays out in a child's entire life. You need a therapist who has a working knowledge of the trauma your kiddos have endured before coming into your care.

4. Do they listen first and respond second? A key indicator of an effective therapist is their ability to listen first before responding. Are they able to give you space to share, express, vent, or unload without interrupting or jumping in with advice? Parents know when something isn't right. You need a therapist who can listen to you and learn what you are seeing in your home with your child.

5. Will they help you build a bond that wasn't there when you first adopted your child? Your primary job is to work to build a bond with your child that wasn't there when you adopted him or her. Any professional you work with should help strengthen this bond.

6. Do they respond appropriately to your child? Not long ago, Kristin took one of our children to an office near where we live for a counseling session. During the appointment, the person conducting the session, who was an adoptee herself, projected her own adoption trauma onto our child. Not appropriate. Our child was confused. Rightfully so. Our child kept correcting the counselor by saying, "That's not what I said." Our child left the appointment frustrated and feeling that he hadn't been heard.

You must find a therapist who can respond appropriately to your child and your child's diagnosis. You must interview them. Schedule an initial visit with them and make it clear that you're trying to find the right person. Then go down the list of questions we just posed. Ask them about their background. Ask for references. Talk about their previous experience in working with children in foster care or who have been adopted. You will quickly learn whether this person understands you and your journey.

39: What should I do when our child acts out and needs discipline?

MIKE | Your child is going to make mistakes, act out, and require you to set healthy boundaries. Every human being will eventually grow up with their own ideals and view of the world. All children need discipline. However, your discipline and boundaries are going to look extremely different from those of traditional parents. Here's what you can do to parent children who have come from a past of trauma:

1. Listen. Listening first can give you an entirely new perspective on a situation with your child. As you listen, quietly ask yourself what is really going on with your child. A key question I often ask myself is, "Do I want to be right, or do I want to be connected?" I've found that this question changes my attitude and opens me up to understand what our child is saying.

2. Set limits. Children thrive when they live within boundaries. Chaos breeds chaos. This is exponentially greater when our children have come from places of trauma.

Disrespect is never to be tolerated. Remain calm but firm. If there's disrespect, calmly and firmly respond by saying, "I would be happy to discuss this with you when you stop calling me names," or "I understand that you would like to watch television. That will happen once you've stopped screaming at me."

3. Redirect. When we're talking about kiddos from hard places, their brains can often fixate on one scenario or one ideal. When this happens, meltdowns and extreme behavior can result if they're not receiving the answer they're looking for. For example, your child may say, "When is dinner? I'm hungry. When is dinner? I'm hungry! I'm not getting enough food…there's no food…I'm starving…I'M STARVING!" This seems like an extreme reaction to mild hunger, but our children may have experienced significant food insecurity.

Redirection can change this significantly. And it's simple—when your child asks, "When is dinner? I'm hungry," recognize that they are feeling hungry and are about to be triggered by survival instincts. You can respond, "I can see you're feeling hungry. Dinner is about to be ready at five. It's four thirty now. Would you like an apple as a snack?" Or, "We're getting close to dinnertime, but I need some help with a few things. Could you cut up this fruit? You can have a few pieces if you want." Redirection works wonders in changing the course of our children's brains.

4. *Connection before correction.* Our traditional parenting experience and instincts prompt us to immediately jump to correction when one of our children acts out or shows disrespect. When we're talking about parenting children from places of trauma, their misbehavior and disrespect carries a reason. Something is fueling their attitude and emotions. Therefore it's critical that we take on a connection approach before we jump to correction.

5. *Safety first.* This really should be the first on the list, but we've found that most of the time, immediate safety is not in question. Safety always comes first. So if your child is up on the roof teetering toward the edge, calmly invite them down off the roof or go get them, and then focus on connection.

6. *Stay calm and remain firm.* Your reaction, tone, and emotions have the power to heighten a child's emotions and behavior or de-escalate them. We can often become a trigger for our children if we don't keep ourselves under control.

7. *Pay attention to timing.* Sometimes a consequence needs to happen right away, but sometimes it should come later. We often jump the gun on timing because we've allowed our emotions to get the best of us. If we're not careful, we end up overreacting or reacting too early.

8. *Allow natural consequences.* Sometimes the best way to discipline your child is to lovingly and calmly encourage them. If your child misses the bus, encourage them to walk or ride their bike. If your child has to stay after school for detention, offer to pick them up later but do not undermine the school's process. If your child leaves their shoes out by the trampoline, remind them once to bring them in but do not do it for them. And if the police show up at the door, cooperate with the authorities.

40: How can I encourage my family and close friends to support our parenting style?

KRISTIN | Once we know the importance attachment and bonding play in a healthy upbringing, we tend to parent differently. Children from traumatic pasts have had their initial attachment disrupted, so we must parent intentionally to teach our children healthy skills to build trust. We must form a sturdy support system around them. Most people will get on board with our parenting style, but sometimes even our close family and friends don't understand why we do what we do. Some will intentionally sabotage our efforts, while others will unintentionally disrupt the bond we are building with our child. Whatever the motivation behind the behavior of the adults surrounding our family, we must remain firm.

Usually the biggest threat to our parenting is in the form of seemingly nonthreatening behaviors.

- Aunt Ida just wants to give little Jimmy one more cookie even though Mom said no, so she sneaks him a cookie.

- Uncle Bill loves his nieces and nephews and bear hugs each one before letting them through the door at family gatherings. The nieces and nephews think this tradition is funny—to them it is simply a special part of their relationship with Uncle Bill. But the newly adopted niece, Bella, balks at the tradition and refuses to get out of the car at Thanksgiving dinner.

- The reading recovery teacher always gives her students a treat after class. Johnny experienced food insecurity as a baby, so he asks the teacher every day for an extra treat. The teacher begins bringing a granola bar to school every day for Johnny without telling Mom and Dad what is going on.

- Great-Grandma demands that every child give her a "proper hug" and is cross when Becca responds by standing stiff as a board.

- The next-door neighbor, Bev, believes that newly adopted Sarah is melting down because she is spoiled. When Mom and Dad aren't looking, Bev tells Sarah she better shape up. When Mom and Dad are around, Bev tells them how to parent, speaking so loudly that Sarah can hear her disapproval.

I'm sure you can come up with plenty of scenarios where your community has hindered healthy attachment, bonding, and healing with your child. So what can we do?

1. Invite. First, invite people in your close circle to talk. This should be a nonthreatening conversation. Explain the basics of trauma and your parenting style. This is not the time to tell the child's story—their story is their own to tell, never yours. You can be vague. If the person is receptive, invite them to be a part of the solution. Ask them to look to you for guidance before crossing any of the boundaries you've set.

2. Educate. For those who choose to be a healthy support for your child, education is important. Here are some things you'll want your team to understand.

- *The benefits of healthy attachments.* Healthy attachments lead to healthy relationships. Healthy relationships are the foundation of everything your child will experience in life. Healthy attachments with family will teach the child how to choose safe people in the future. It is within these familial relationships that the child will learn to obey authority, stand up for himself, negotiate, handle disappointment, and experience joy.

- *The dangers of the lack of attachment.* Children who do not learn to attach risk unhealthy relationships in the future. They may trust the wrong people or no one at all. They may be a target for predators who will use their lack of connection to their favor.

- *The warning signs of unhealthy attachment.* Children who have experienced trauma may show signs of detachment

in many ways, such as by being indiscriminately affectionate, withdrawn, rigid, fearful, charming, manipulative, or
explosive. Others may not see the lack of attachment for
what it is, especially if the child is outgoing and charming.
People outside our close circle may mistake the behavior as
a sign that the child is well adjusted rather than a warning
that the child is using a survival tactic.

3. Limit time with those who sabotage the trust you are building. Once
you reach out, invite, and educate those around you, you may find that
some people will continue to sabotage your efforts to build a healthy
relationship with your child. Limit your time with these people.

4. Lean on those who support you and your child. When you find the
group of people who truly support you and your child, lean on them.
They will encourage you as you navigate this journey to building trust.

41: Can we overdo therapeutic parenting?

KRISTIN | "Don't you understand how to work with kids from
trauma?" my nine-year-old screamed at the bus driver, exiting the
doors of the school bus and stepping onto our long driveway. He
turned around and continued, "You have to talk to us in a calm voice!
My brain has flipped right now, and I'm freaking out!" I scurried to
the end of the driveway and stood at the open door of the bus, staring
directly into the bus driver's red face. He was not amused. "Go inside
now," I firmly told our son, and then I apologized to Mr. Bus Driver.

We are proud of our kids for using their words and understanding
their own trauma background, but we were not happy with the way
our son handled the situation on the bus. He was out of his seat while
the bus was speeding down rural back roads. The bus driver had asked
him multiple times to sit down and explained to him that it was about
safety. He finally got angry and yelled at our son to sit down. Our son
struggles with impulsivity and isn't great at dealing with frustrating

situations. He was using his trauma background as a crutch and his trauma knowledge as a weapon.

Therapeutic parenting has strengthened our children in so many ways. We parent better because we understand the role trauma has played in the development of our children's brains. But if we aren't careful, we can overdo it. When we notice our children using our parenting style as a crutch, we need to reevaluate and approach the situation differently.

Let's ask ourselves a few questions about our parenting style to see if we need to tweak what we are doing a bit and approach our children differently.

- Is what I'm doing hindering our child?
- Am I supporting or enabling our child?
- Is our child using our parenting style as an excuse for poor behavior?
- Am I using our child's trauma experience as an excuse?
- Is our child gaining independence because of the approach I'm using?
- Does my approach build our child's confidence?

Part 4

EMPOWERING
CHILDREN

42: Why is it important to empower our children?

KRISTIN | "Ugh!" our daughter sighed at the dinner table after we asked, "How was school today?" She then launched into a story about a girl in her child development class who kept asking her about her "real parents."

Our daughter kept responding, "Well, I have biological parents and adoptive parents, and they are both real."

The girl wasn't taking the hint. Our daughter had experienced this type of conversation throughout her 16 years as an adoptee and a foster child. She is the kind of grace-giving person who assumes the best in others. (Wouldn't it be nice if we could all be that way?) But on this day, she was just completely over the ignorance and exhausted by the rude nosiness.

Foster children have to deal with the feeling of being out of control all the time. They are not able to advocate for themselves about the issue that matters the most—family. Judges, caseworkers, foster parents, birth parents, and other professionals make all the decisions for them. They can't get a haircut, enroll in school, travel outside of the state, visit biological family members, or visit the doctor without having to jump through the hoops of the foster care system. The system is there to keep them safe, but it rarely meets the emotional needs of the children it serves. Children are taken from the only family they've ever known and bounced through a system of care with adults who are often not communicating with one another or listening to the child they are meant to serve.

As foster and adoptive parents, we have a great responsibility not only to advocate for our children but also to pass along the tools our children will need to advocate for themselves throughout life. It's our responsibility to empower our children. They are at a greater disadvantage than others because they don't believe they can be in charge of themselves. During their development as a child, adults have stepped in and made life-altering decisions without their consent.

Our foster or adoptive children do not always have a consistent listening ear that most children have as they process hard things. I learned to care for myself because my parents showed care for me, listened to me, and empowered me. We have to be more conscious with our children about this empowering. In some ways our children will learn these skills naturally, but in other ways they will always doubt that they have control over themselves.

- Children need to learn to use their voice so they will be prepared for the future.

- Children need to learn to take responsibility for themselves by practicing within the safety of their own home.

43: How can I empower our children to face difficult situations?

KRISTIN | Foster care and adoption are difficult. There will be hard parts to our child's story. It is inevitable. Our children will see some things in their past as normal and others as difficult. It isn't for us to decide which parts are difficult for our children. This is why it is so important that our children feel empowered to deal with the hard parts. Here are some things we can do to help:

1. Don't change the story. We must not try to decide the narrative for them. Only our children know the perspective from which they see things. If we are to empower our children to process their own story, we must first let them tell the story.

2. Ask questions. Children may not know it's okay to share the difficult parts of what they are feeling. Ask open-ended questions and allow your child to decide the direction: "If you could ask your birth mom one thing, what would you ask?" Your child may respond by wondering about her favorite candy bar or wondering why she left and didn't come back. Open-ended questions allow your child to take the conversation in whatever direction they want it to go.

3. Listen without interruption. No matter what, allow your child to tell the whole story. This can be so hard when we know the adult version of what happened. Our children may believe their mom is a princess or their dad would never make them do chores. It's hard not to step in and change the narrative. There is danger in believing the fantasy, but there is more danger in never allowing your child to think the entire scenario through in the first place. They will process reality at some point. Our job is to listen.

On the other hand, our child may share a very dark version of their story. They may say something like, "I'm just worthless. No one came back for me." This is an even harder narrative not to interrupt. It is still our job to listen to the whole thing. Let your child sit in the hard emotion while you listen and support from the sideline. You cannot take this emotion away by interrupting the story here. Allow your child to tell all of what they are feeling. Prompt with more open-ended questions if necessary, but allow your child to work through the whole feeling.

4. Support no matter what. As our children process the hard parts, we can support through our actions, words, and body language. If a child lashes out at us while processing, it's okay to say, "Please don't say that word to me," or "I love you no matter what," or "I know you are feeling angry." If our child is crying, it's okay to let them know you feel sad too, but reassure them that you are strong enough to handle any emotion they are having and that they do not have to hide it from you. You may need to confide in a friend about your own emotions after your child processes something hard, but while your child is processing, this is the time to support no matter what.

5. Provide a safe, neutral place to process. I'll be the first to admit that I want to know everything our children are thinking, talking about, and feeling. That isn't healthy. Actively seek out a counselor who understands trauma and attachment. Having a neutral counselor will give your children a safe space and empower them to process the hard parts without Mom and Dad present. An adult adoptee can help our children see that their emotions are very normal. A group of friends who have been adopted or spent time in foster care can provide a community where our children can feel like they can let their guard down and talk without always having to explain the backstory.

44: How can I empower our children to process the good parts of their story?

KRISTIN | Celebration seems like a normal part of our humanity, but for children who have experienced great loss, the ability to celebrate isn't a given. Have you ever met a person who seems to sabotage every good thing? Do you know someone who avoids family gatherings, such as Thanksgiving or Christmas? How about someone who always seems to see the glass half empty? The child who cannot seem to relax and have a good time may simply not know how.

When I think of my childhood, I remember waiting for Christmas morning with palpable anticipation. When the morning arrived, I burst out of my bed and waited patiently on the stairs with my brothers and sister. I knew every detail of our traditions, and I didn't want to miss one. I relished in the slow opening of each gift. I felt overjoyed at the sight of each item—even socks were a wonder! I knew how to enjoy the moment. I had no reason to believe that it wouldn't be a wonderful day, and it always was.

One of our children avoids Christmas like the plague. Before the day even starts, there is complaining and preemptive disappointment. It seems ungrateful and downright rude, but when we dig a little deeper, we notice something else. This child's inability to celebrate stems from years of real disappointment and lack of follow-through. They're not trying to ruin the day, but it always seems to end up that way. Our children need permission and empowerment to celebrate. They need to know it's okay to relax, let their guard down, and enjoy the good things in life.

1. Talk about it. So often we forget to include our children in the conversation and the solution. If we are going to empower them to grow up to be healthy adults, we must trust them first with the conversation. Start by saying, "Your birthday is coming up. I know this can sometimes be a hard time for you. Why do you think that is?" Then listen. Engage in the conversation about the why first and then invite the child to give some ideas on how he or she would feel comfortable celebrating.

One of our children becomes agitated when our living space is disrupted by the Christmas tree, lights, wrapping paper, and everything else involved with Christmas. He doesn't feel like he can settle down and enjoy the day amid the mess. Once we talked about it with him, we were able to come up with a solution to help him enjoy the day and celebrate in his own way.

Another child feels the pressure to act happy on special days regardless of how she really feels. We now celebrate in a different way with her on a different day.

2. Model celebration. I like things to be neat, orderly, tidy. It can be hard for me to settle down and enjoy special days and celebrations. If you are having a hard time enjoying the joyful moments in life, take time to plan ahead for the special day. Allow your children to see you relax and experience joy as well.

45: How can we empower children with two families to embrace their own identity?

KRISTIN | We are a multiracial, multigenerational, multicultural family. We have our own identity as a family, and it is unique to us. It includes the things we laugh at, the movies we watch, our traditions, and our inside jokes. It includes a set of values and expectations we live by. This is a very important part of our identity, but it is not our entire identity.

In any family, two separate units join under one roof. In an adoptive family, each person brings a little piece of something else to the table. In our home, we are African, Scottish, Irish, German, and Italian. We have lived in trailers, apartments, large homes, and tiny homes. We have lived in rural areas, urban areas, and suburban areas. When we come together, each person brings his or her own history. Our identity is a compilation of all that makes us who we are. It is the label we put on ourselves.

All children are trying to find their place in the world. It is in our DNA to discover who we really are. For children who are adopted, the possibilities for identity are endless. All people tug and push and pull at the things that define us throughout life. My identity is different than it was when I was twenty, and it is different from when I was ten. Parents can support children as they find and embrace their own identities. We can empower them to see value in themselves in all circumstances. Here's how:

1. Ask. We empower our children by asking questions that help them think on their own. A simple question, such as "What do you think about that?" allows our children to value their own opinion. Asking "Why do you think that?" helps your child stretch their ability to think through things.

2. Listen. Listen to the answer even if it is not exactly what you want to hear. Listen even if it's not exactly who you are. If your child embraces the culture of their birth, listen. If they are walking, talking, dressing, or thinking like a group of people they identify with, listen. Be open as they find where they fit in.

3. Offer exposure to like-minded people. Especially in transracial adoptive families, exposure to people who are similar to our children is vital. Our children should see themselves reflected in the people around them. We can help by exposing our children to people who look and talk like them. If your child speaks a different first language, provide a place for them to use the language of their birth. If your child is from a rural area and you have moved to an urban area, allow your child to spend time in the country.

4. *Embrace them.* Children learn self-empowerment when the adults in their lives embrace them. If the child loves science, embrace that. If the child is a social butterfly, embrace that. Let your child know you delight in them no matter what. Assure your child that no matter where they fit in society, they will always fit in your home and your family. A solid identity comes first from a solid foundation at home.

46: How can we teach our kids how to advocate for their own needs?

KRISTIN | Last week I attended our daughter's Meet the Teacher Night at her high school. I got a copy of her schedule and proceeded to her first class. Each class met for seven minutes so the teacher could give a brief introduction and overview. The first class was advanced-placement government. I can tell you right now that it is only through the miracle of adoption that Mike and I have a child in an advanced-placement class. The teacher began by explaining that this is a college-level class. She has given the students all the tools they need to succeed in the class, and she expects that her students will exhaust every possible way of communicating and advocating for themselves before a parent gets involved. I nodded and smiled, feeling grateful that our daughter had a teacher who would push her to grow in her own advocacy this year.

The first test came after only seven days of school. Our daughter failed a test after studying for days. I was heartbroken for her. She cried and then threw her hands up and exclaimed she was going to quit. I suggested she email the teacher and set up a time to go in for extra help during the teacher's study hour. She refused and went to bed. I sighed, thinking that hadn't gone as planned. But the next morning before I had even gotten out of bed, our daughter had already set up a time to get extra help. That's when she learned that 95 percent of the class failed the test. She had a plan to do better, and she had come up with it herself!

Advocacy is something we will do our entire lives. For foster and adoptive children, they will have to advocate for themselves even more often. They will face unwanted attention, questions, and assumptions. They may need accommodations in school and in the workplace due to disabilities caused by the trauma of neglect, disruption, attachment disorder, drug and alcohol exposure, and more. It can be overwhelming to advocate for our children, so how can we teach them to do it for themselves? When we see our children's struggles or insecurities, we often want to take the struggle away because we think they have suffered enough without having to answer another insensitive question or deal with another unkind teacher. We simply can't step in forever. The best gift we can give our children is the confidence and skills to advocate for themselves. Here are some ideas that will help:

1. *Begin early.* Teaching our children to advocate for themselves begins early. We can encourage children to use age-appropriate skills. Teach an infant to use baby sign language. Allow a preschooler to choose his or her own outfit. Elementary-age kids can help create a system for school organization or pack their own lunch. Middle schoolers can arrange their own social activities and keep a calendar of practices and appointments. High schoolers can begin to navigate extracurricular activities, part-time jobs, and relationships with minimal guidance from adults.

2. *Don't do everything for them.* I'll admit, this is hard for me. I kind of enjoy packing lunches and folding laundry. I am much faster at household chores, and I can type our child's paper much faster than he can (and with much less complaining). Don't do this. Self-confidence and self-sufficiency lead to self-advocacy. Children will learn to get help meeting their needs when they know what they need.

3. *Include them in deciding what they need to be successful.* When our son was in first grade, his teacher had flexible seating in her classroom. I asked her, "How do you get the kids to choose a seat that helps them learn instead of one that distracts them?" She told me she spends about a week teaching the children about their bodies and learning

styles before allowing them to choose where to sit. She then used open-ended questions to encourage them throughout the year to make good choices: "I see you have been bouncing a lot in this chair. Do you feel like you are able to stay focused, or is it time to choose a new seat?" The children in her classroom were empowered to advocate for themselves and identify their specific learning needs.

We can do this at home. What things help your child sleep? What type of clothes do they prefer? Are they sensitive to light, sound, texture, taste? Teach them to be aware of their own bodies and needs. Teach solutions and problem-solving skills. Allow your child to find the best way to address his or her needs.

One of our sons doesn't like his pants to touch his ankles. We could roll his pants for him forever, or we could teach him to roll his own pants. Our son is now ten years old and still chooses to wear shorts or pants rolled up at the cuff. Mike and I haven't had to solve his problem of discomfort in years.

4. *Allow them to fail.* Our daughter first advocated for herself outside of our home in kindergarten. She arrived on the first day to find that kindergarten actually started the next day. (I don't want to talk about how terrible Mike and I felt when we realized our mistake.) She was armed with the tools she needed. She knew her phone number, parents' names, teacher's name, and directions on how to get to her class. She was not paralyzed by fear. She found an adult, explained who she was, and waited for the teacher to contact us. Amazing!

In middle school, this same brilliant child went through a phase of neglecting to turn in her homework. She did the work but didn't turn it in. (Insert deep sigh.) She failed the first quarter of that class. We talked with the teacher and with our daughter and collectively agreed that she was capable of completing the work and capable of creating a system for storing the completed work in her backpack so she wouldn't forget to turn it in. We gave her the tools and pointed her in the right direction. The adults then stepped back. Our daughter talked with the teacher, apologized, came up with a new plan, and even received some extra-credit assignments to bring her grade back up. Mom, Dad, and the teacher agreed to ask her how she was doing with her plan but not intervene.

To our wonder and amazement, she turned the behavior around, used her new system, and even took pride in turning her work in. Allowing her to fail was hard, but it was not the end of the world—it was a stepping-stone to more mature advocacy for herself.

5. *Allow them to try again.* When a child first expresses a need, they may do it inappropriately. When we adults can recognize the behavior as an unmet need, we can help the child try again. Communicate with your child about their feelings. Help your child identify their needs. Begin by helping your child identify their feelings: "It looks like you are feeling sad." As your child grows, they will be able to verbalize their feelings independently. Set boundaries around the behavior: "You may not throw yourself on the floor." Then allow them to try again: "What can you do instead?"

6. *Respect your child.* When a child uses their skills to advocate for themselves, listen and respect them. If a child is requesting something reasonable, such as pants with cuffs at the bottom, it's okay to say yes. Listen to what your child is struggling with and remain interested in the solution. Your child is practicing with you for a time when he or she will need to advocate for something much bigger than comfortable clothes.

7. *Model advocacy.* Allow your child to hear you as you advocate for yourself and others. Invite your child to talk with you about the solutions you are coming up with for problems. As they grow they will be able to attend IEP meetings where they will hear you advocate for their needs. Treat others with respect, listen, and problem solve with an open mind. You are modeling the advocacy your child will one day use on their own.

47: How can I empower our children to own their own stories?

KRISTIN | Our children's stories are their own to tell. This may sound odd coming from an adoptive parent who writes about adoption for a living, so I'll address how we handle this in our own home.

You will notice that we often use vague language when referring to our children. We may say "she" or "he," but we do not use the child's name unless we have clear permission from the child to do so. We use the same process when people ask questions about our family. Sometimes someone wants to know what a child's favorite toy is so they can pick out a birthday gift. We're happy to share that information. If someone wants to know where our kids were adopted from, we may respond by naming the state but not including the city. Someone may push a little more and want to know if the kids were in foster care. This is where we stop answering for our children. We may say that six of our children were adopted from foster care and two were adopted privately. We are willing to talk about our nine years as foster parents but not about what brought each child into our home.

How should foster and adoptive kids talk about their story? Here are a few things to consider as you decide:

1. Practice. From the time a child is small, allow them to practice answering questions at home. Let them know they do not have to answer anything about themselves—ever. Remind them that their private story is their own and not for anyone else to know. Give them tools to end conversations that become intrusive. Also help them find the words to tell their story in the way they feel comfortable.

2. Let the child decide. Who are the safe people in a child's life? Who can they talk to about their story? How do they determine who is a good person to talk to? Tell your child how you determine who is a trustworthy friend in your own life and what you have done in the past if you found out a person wasn't as trustworthy as you first thought.

3. Guide. You cannot make your child say or do anything, but you can guide your child. Help them learn to tell their own story in a way that makes them feel confident. Remind them that they do not ever have to share a part of themselves with anyone else. Guide them through scenarios they may face. Be there to listen when they encounter something unexpected.

4. Model. Set boundaries around yourself and your child. Allow your child to listen in as you tell the parts that are okay and keep other parts private. Let your child hear you say, "That's private" when someone asks an intrusive question. Tell your own story selectively and talk with your children about why some people are more trustworthy than others. For instance, my kids know that their dad and I talk about everything, that we have no secrets with each other, and that we are partners. They know that my mom knows almost everything, that she supports and loves our family unconditionally, and that she never gossips, so she is a safe person to talk to. They know that the next-door neighbors get to know a very small portion of information about our family. Keep your child's story private. Your child should never find out something about themselves from anyone but you or their birth family.

48: How can I empower our child to have their own relationship with biological family members?

KRISTIN | I can hear it right now: "Yes, but…" I know that not all biological family members are safe or healthy for our children. I know that not every situation lends itself easily to open adoption. I also know that curious children will go after things they have been denied, especially relationships with their family of origin. Our children will only be children for 18 years. That is a simple fact. At age 18, they may decide for themselves what their relationships with biological family members will be. It is our job to empower them with the skills to make healthy decisions about all relationships before they have to navigate them on their own. Here's how:

1. *Model.* Show your children what healthy relationships look like in your own life. Set healthy boundaries with your friends and your own extended family members.

2. *Talk.* Converse with your children about how to have healthy relationships and what makes a good supportive relationship. Talk with your children about what they hope their relationship looks like with biological family members and what they plan to do if the relationship doesn't turn out the way they hope.

3. Listen. Hear your child's thoughts, hopes, dreams, and fears. Allow them the space to process with you. Don't interrupt. Listen until it's your turn to talk. Listen with an open heart.

4. Assist. You can be the foundation for your child as they search for their birth family and build relationships with them. Allow your child to navigate his or her relationship with their birth family and be confident that you have taught your child how to set good boundaries. Be there to assist but don't insert yourself into your child's relationships.

5. Be confident. Your child's relationship with their birth family is not an attack on you. It isn't about you—it's about your child. You may feel many emotions alongside your child, and that's okay. Rejoice when they rejoice and grieve when they grieve. This relationship is not something that will minimize your own relationship with your child. It's an opportunity for growth for both you and your child as you embrace new members of your family.

49: How can I empower our child to love and care for himself?

KRISTIN | People learn to love themselves by first experiencing the love of a parent. When attachment is broken, a child feels it to their core. It shapes how they view themselves and their worth. The process to healing this loss can take a lifetime. The healing starts with you.

1. Show love to your child no matter what. Respond with love. Even when setting boundaries, set them with an attitude of love. Let your child know that certain behaviors are not okay because they are harmful, unsafe, and so on. Explain why a boundary is there. You may say, "I can't drive this car until you have your seat belt buckled. I love you and I want you to be safe." When a child reacts with emotions of anger, frustration, or fear, respond with love. You can say, "I see that you are angry. I love you—what can I do to help you work through this?"

2. Set a healthy example of caring for yourself. It seems like the most loving thing you can do for another person is to put them first. But one of the most loving things you can do for your child is to first care for yourself. You are at your best when you have had a good night's sleep, healthy food, and some time alone. Lead your children by example— take care of yourself because they are watching.

3. *Allow your child to direct their own self-care.* They may like time alone in their room, or they may be filled up by sitting right smack in the middle of a roomful of people. Verbalize what you are seeing and let your child choose ways to take care of themselves. If your child likes to read, bake, run, or watch television, talk with them about these things and set aside time in each day to do something they love. Point out the things you witness and encourage them to brainstorm other ways to care for themselves.

One of our sons hates vegetables. We want him to eat healthy foods, so we invite him into the meal planning. He will even participate in hiding spinach inside of a fruit smoothie! He knows it's there, and he wants to take care of himself, but he also knows he doesn't like the way it tastes unless it's covered up with frozen peaches and strawberries. He will grow into an adult who can care for himself because he is already practicing ways to do that now.

4. *Encourage positive conversations about unique traits.* We delight in the uniqueness of our children, and they need to know it. If the world were made up of only one type of person, we would be in big trouble. Families are the same.

One of our children loves to bake. It makes her feel relaxed and filled with joy. She loves to share baked good with others, thus sharing the feeling of joy. One of our children loves to read, write, and tell stories. Long drives feel shorter when the child shares his funny, wild, and creative tall tales. Children will learn to love themselves when they are certain they are loved at home. They will value their unique talents and gifts when they know those traits are valued at home.

50: What can I do to help our child endure disappointment?

KRISTIN | We sat outside of the visitation center two towns away from our own home. The rough concrete stairs had begun to make my backside feel numb. My foster daughter sat beside me silently, looking away toward the empty parking lot. Our own car was parked on the street, and I longed to make a run for it. I sneaked a glance at my watch—her mom was 23 minutes late. I didn't dare look at the face of the hurting child beside me, so I fixed my eyes on my own freckled knees.

After 30 minutes on the dot, the visitation supervisor cracked the door and waited for me to make eye contact. I looked up, and he shook his head. "You can go now." Our daughter and I didn't respond as we rose and walked toward our van. She climbed into the back bench seat and buckled her seat belt. I turned the key and ventured a glance at her in the rearview mirror. A tear slipped from her closed eyes and I turned my attention back to the road. "Ice cream?" I asked quietly, and she nodded yes. And this was our pattern. Disappointment and then a trip to Dairy Queen. We would order our Heath Blizzards and sit in silence until things felt a little better. When we were connected again, we threw our trash away and headed home.

Over and over, we watch our children experience disappointment. As parents, this is just something we do. They won't make every team. They won't pass every test. They won't be invited to every birthday party. Not every teacher will like them. For foster and adopted children, the disappointment can feel personal. They may internalize a missed visit or an inappropriately nosey stranger as a reflection of themselves. As adoptive and foster parents, we can feel helpless as our children navigate their own identity in the context of relinquishment, abandonment, or a neglected relationship.

Disappointment is a reality. There are some things we can do when disappointment strikes:

1. Do not rescue your child from their emotions. When our child internalizes a disappointment, I am so often tempted to say, "Oh honey, that isn't true," or "I'm sure there was just a misunderstanding," or some such phrase, hoping to soften the blow. Don't do that. You cannot stop your child from feeling the hard emotions. When you try, you rob them from the full circle of that emotion. When they work through the entire emotion, they will be able to accept the positive emotions that come back around.

2. Listen without interruption. Listen to the entire thought, rage, or expression of sadness. It can be so difficult not to step in when a child says something like, "She missed a visit again. I'm worthless—I'm a piece of trash." It's hard to hear something like that come out of the mouth of someone you love, but let them finish the entire thought.

3. Be patient. Not all children process verbally. Be patient as your child works through his or her emotions in their own way. It's okay for your child to sit silently, read a book, sit in their room, or take a walk. Periodically invite your child back into the routine of family life and back into healthy conversation.

4. Be persistent. You set the tone for how your child feels about the disappointment. Give your child space but be sure to return to the subject. This may mean making a special trip to get a milkshake and talk or having a conversation as you tuck the child in with only the nightlight on.

5. Seek counseling. Find counselors in your area who are experienced with cases of adoption and trauma. Ask friends, online communities, and local foster and adoption agencies for recommendations.

6. Be honest. Don't create a fantasy to soften the blow of disappointment. If Mom missed another visit, don't lie about it. Tell the truth in all things. Chances are, your child already knows. When you tell the truth about the hard stuff, your child is more likely to believe you when you encourage them with the good stuff.

7. Be encouraging. Tell your child how you feel about them. It doesn't replace the disappointment, but there is nothing better than hearing that someone loves, values, and adores you. It is important to remember that your words of love may be met with eye rolls and sighs, but that's okay! Keep saying it.

8. Seek support for your child. Adoptees need other adoptees. Find support groups with children their age. Find adult adoptees and invite them to be a part of your community. Your child needs people who have had the same life experiences.

9. Seek support for yourself. You need adoptive parents to share this experience with. You will be a better parent when you have someone you can share ideas with and learn from. You need one trusted someone to share the heartache over your child's disappointment. This person must be trustworthy and must care for your child as you do. Finding connection as parents strengthens our ability to parent.

51: How can I empower our child to grieve?

KRISTIN | Our children often hesitate to show and share emotion because they have not had a safe place to do that in the past. They may keep hard parts of their story from us because they are afraid we will think less of them, we will think less of their first family, or we will not be able to handle the knowledge of the sad things. Our children often try to protect us by not showing their grief. Grief cannot be healed unless we first acknowledge that it exists. So…

1. Model healthy expressions of grief. Everyone will experience loss and disappointment in life. When you do, allow your child to see you process it in a healthy way.

2. Give space for grief. When your child grieves, allow them to have space to do so. They will feel all types of emotions in connection with their loss. All emotions are valid. Giving your children space to work through each emotion and feeling will help them in the future to address feelings of loss and grief.

3. Identify triggers. These emotions may be triggered by unrelated things such as the move to a new house or a certain time of year, a smell, sound, sight, or taste. Helping your child know the triggers and where they come from will be a tool that will empower them to handle feelings of grief in the future.

4. Teach coping skills. Teaching your child tools to use in moments of intense feeling will help them cope in the future in all types of situations. For example, kids can draw pictures, write in a diary, learn new ways to describe their feelings, find mementos that have special meaning for them, participate in ceremonies that commemorate the loss, and so on.

52: How can I empower our child to build healthy attachments?

KRISTIN | Children attach to a caregiver as a natural part of their development. A child will attach first with his or her mother, then the father, and then consistent caregivers such as a grandmother, big sister, or aunt. The child will build this ability to trust and practice it in day-care, preschool, or kindergarten. As the child grows, they will form different levels of attachment to friends, coaches, teachers, and eventually a spouse and children. When that first attachment is disrupted, a domino effect happens with future attachments.

Here are some ideas for helping kids learn how to build healthy attachments:

1. *Be patient.* Attachment will take time. Allow your child to take as much time as needed (maybe even 30 years). Allowing this attachment to happen as naturally as possible will empower your child to lead the way in making attachments to others in his or her future.

2. *Be consistent.* You remain the same even though your child will draw close and push away throughout childhood and possibly into adulthood as well. This is natural for all children, but for our children, it can feel magnified. Stand strong as a parent. Love unconditionally.

3. *Learn methods for attachment.* Work with a therapist who specializes in attachment, bonding, and trauma. Read about attachment. We recommend *The Connected Child* by Karen Purvis. Find what your child needs and seeks out. Your attachment strategies will vary depending on age and personality. As you learn, teach your child. They will need these strategies if they are to be empowered to bond with their friends and future spouse and children.

53: How can I empower our child to utilize resources as he or she grows older?

KRISTIN | As your children grow, they take on more responsibility. When I was a senior in high school, I needed a dentist appointment. My mom handed me the phone and showed me the page in the address book with the dentist's number. She was teaching me to use my resources. In foster care and adoption, our children will need to know how to use resources that others may not. They may need to know how to find a counselor, how to obtain assistance at college, or how to research and locate information about their biological family history. Here are some ways you can teach them to handle responsibilities like these:

1. Start early. Teach your child to ask a grocery store employee where the mac and cheese is. Allow your child to call a friend and set up a playdate. As the child matures, allow them to set up a doctor's appointment or help choose a therapist they like.

2. Teach the language. Children need to know how to explain their medical history, family history, and medical and mental health diagnoses. When we teach our children the proper language to use, they will be empowered to communicate their needs well as adults.

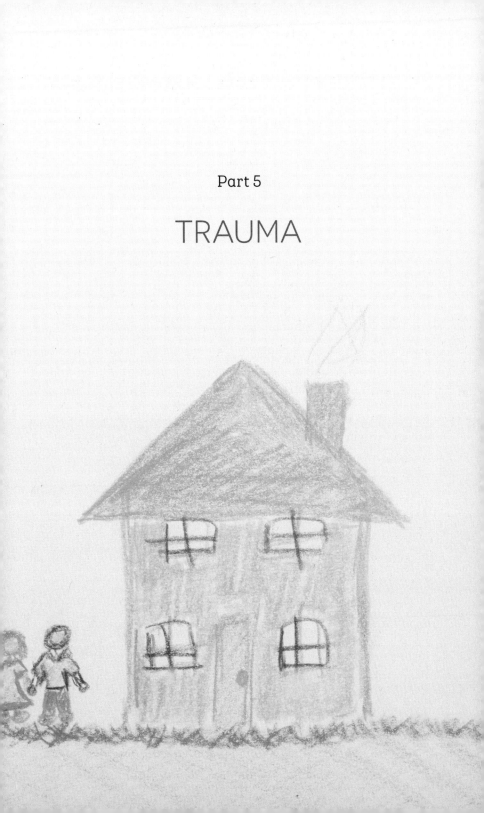

Part 5

TRAUMA

54: How will understanding our child's trauma help me as a parent?

MIKE | I will never forget the moment my mind was fully opened to the reality of what our children have experienced and why they do and say the things they do. It was Christmastime, four years ago. On a cold December night, something triggered our oldest son, who is diagnosed with alcohol-related neurodevelopmental disorder (commonly called ARND, a fetal alcohol spectrum disorder, or FASD). We were popping popcorn, pulling out blankets, and settling down in our family room for a family movie night. For reasons that remain a mystery, he wasn't having any of it.

The movie was the wrong movie, the popcorn was too salty, his sister looked at him, he thought movie night was stupid, he hated this family, and he wished it wasn't Christmas break so he could go back to school. On and on and on until finally he lunged at his younger brother and tried to punch him. In our home, when someone displays behaviors that become unsafe or threatening, we remove them from the room, and Kristin or I spend time alone with them.

I was frustrated and couldn't see the full reality of our son's behavior that night. As he lay facedown in our upstairs bathroom, screaming obscenities, I fumed. I opened my mouth to say, "If you don't knock this crap off, I'm gonna..." but was suddenly stopped in my tracks. In that moment my eyes were fully opened, and the veil was torn away. I realized he wasn't a bad kid being bad. He was a scared kid voicing his unmet needs through this outburst.

That night changed the way we approached our kiddos and how we saw their world. Suddenly we saw what was really going on with them. We realized they were voicing something we couldn't understand. Understanding how chronic trauma plays out in a human being's life gave us a brand-new perspective. And boy oh boy, did the adoptive journey change for us.

Fully understanding chronic trauma and how it changes the brain can transform your entire journey. Here's why:

1. *You'll respond to the world around you in a new way.* That child in your neighborhood who bullies the other kids. The little girl in your son's class who hangs upside down in her seat. Suddenly you start to understand that this may not be a bad kid behaving badly, but rather an unmet need being voiced from a place you know nothing about.

When I learned that chronic trauma hinders the use of logic and reasoning and instead propels the person into survival mode, I saw many everyday interactions in a new light. I can now see people with compassion and understanding.

2. *Your heart will break.* Annette Breaux, a bestselling author and sought-after speaker, wrote, "Nine times out of ten, the story behind the misbehavior won't make you angry, it will break your heart." So, so true! When you understand how trauma impacts your children, you become compassionate. That has changed the way we interact with our son.

3. *You will parent differently.* I used to respond angrily to our son's outbursts. I was annoyed when he would impulsively ask the same question over and over again. My own anxiety would heighten when he quickly jumped from one thing to the other. I've learned to respond differently now. Once I understood what his past trauma did to his brain functionality, I began to respond calmly, understanding that my heightened emotion would also heighten his.

I also used to struggle to understand how, even after being in our home for more than ten years, he still melted down over what I considered "normal" things, such as our daily schedule or household rules. A child who's gone through chronic trauma, even at a very young age, has learned to function from a place of survival, often absent from logic or reasoning. If they've gone through this neglect over a long period of time, it may be years before they learn to trust and connect in a healthy manner. This knowledge helped me adjust my expectations with my own children.

4. You will move into action. I believe understanding and knowledge can lead directly to advocacy. When my heart breaks, my feet move. Over the past four years, I've grown to fully appreciate how our knowledge of the way trauma impacts our kiddos can change the world.

If you have been in the dark like I once was, it's okay. Step into the light. Look at your precious kiddo in a new light. Now take one step in front of the other from this moment forward.

55: What should I do if I feel afraid of our child's birth family?

MIKE | I'll never forget the day fear became a regular part of my life as a foster and adoptive parent. We had just wrapped up a hearing on the permanency status of one our children (then in foster care). We were walking out of the courthouse with our child's birth mother and her husband when they stopped us in the middle of the parking lot, looked us dead in the eye, and said bluntly, "Don't allow [the birth father] anywhere near you, your house, or your family. Don't tell him where you live. He will see what you have, kick your door in, and take it from you—including the baby."

As I type these words, I can still remember the way I felt when they told us this. My body instantly filled with anxiety. There was a pounding sensation in my head, and my hands became cold and clammy. I had that out-of-control feeling the entire drive back to our house that afternoon.

The constant state of anxiety continued for about five or six months. Every single day I woke up feeling afraid, fearing a person I had never actually met face-to-face. The fear was crippling. My fear of the birth parent started to affect the way I functioned. Finally a good friend spoke truth into my life, and I suddenly found myself asking a very big question: "What are you really afraid of?"

On Saturday, March 4, 1933, Franklin D. Roosevelt spoke these iconic words during his inauguration as the thirty-second president of the United States: "We have nothing to fear but fear itself." This quote has been recited during times of war. It has been repeated by politicians and government officials in times of world crisis or terror. We see it branded on signs during natural disasters and social unrest. These words have made their way into our homes and our hearts. But what was FDR really saying on that cold winter day in 1933? I believe he was warning us that if we give fear enough power, attention, or authority, it won't hesitate to start controlling everything we think and do.

There are times we need to be afraid, but I've found that they are exceptions, not the rule. After adopting eight children and fostering twenty-three others, I've discovered that I rarely have anything to fear. We often allow ourselves to think the worst before we really know the facts. We instinctively allow fear to take up residence. To break this unhelpful response, ask yourself these four questions:

1. What are the cold, hard facts? Find out what the facts are surrounding a case. It's okay to read police reports or court documents. Take time to weed through opinions and sort out the facts.

2. What are others saying about this person? Be careful with this one because not everyone's opinion will be accurate. If you have a reason to suspect this person is not safe, ask professionals who have been involved in the case. Reach out to case managers or law enforcement officers who are familiar with the case and ask if he or she is a safe person.

3. Can we talk? If you can, have a conversation with your child's birth family and believe the best until you are forced to do otherwise. You will usually discover that your fears are unfounded.

4. Am I safe? This is a very important question to ask at the end of the day. Not "Do I feel safe?" but rather "Am I safe?" Feelings are important but not always based on reality. "Am I safe?" is based on the facts.

As people of faith, we lean heavily on Romans 12:18: "As far as it depends on you, live at peace with everyone." You cannot control others, but you can control yourself. You are responsible for the "as far as it depends on you" part of this verse. Do everything in your power to live at peace with everyone until you have a legitimate reason not to.

The story at the beginning of this chapter ends better than I thought it would. Guess why? We talked to him! We met with him face-to-face and learned about him, his struggles, his hopes, and his dreams. You can learn a lot about a person when you take the time to really get to know them.

56: Should I talk about our child's past trauma with them?

MIKE | "Oh my gosh, stop eating like that…it's not like you're starving!" belted out our daughter as one of our sons shoveled spaghetti and meatballs onto his spoon and into his mouth with barely a breath in between. Spaghetti and meatballs has always been one of his favorite meals. That explained some of the shoveling but not all.

"Why are you talking to him like that?" Kristin asked calmly. Our daughter paused and stared in my wife's direction, searching for an answer. None came.

"Do you know what's happened to him?" she continued gently while our son continued to eat. "Do you know what he went through in his early life to cause him to eat like that? He doesn't do it on purpose." Our daughter nodded as Kristin calmly explained our son's traumatic past to her. She then softly reminded our son that there's plenty of food and he wouldn't go hungry.

A little while later, we explained a few things to our daughter: "It's like you forgetting things repeatedly," I said. "Do you know why that happens? You're forgetful but you also went through some pretty hard stuff a long time ago that has affected the way you think at times."

For the next several minutes, we sat together around our dining room table and talked openly about where she'd come from and the trauma she went through before coming into our care at age three. Understanding washed over her face. It was healthy and affirming, and it helped our child know that we were in this fight with her, not against her.

Here are some rules we follow when we're discussing our child's diagnosis or traumatic past with them or with them in earshot:

1. Be honest but cautious with details. We are honest with our children when they ask questions. We talk about what they went through, but we proceed with caution when it comes to specifics, keeping in mind their age and stage of life and silently asking ourselves if they are ready for these kinds of details.

2. Be honest but respectful of birth parents. We believe in talking about birth parents with dignity and honor. They're human, and so are we. Balance honesty with dignity and respect.

3. Be honest but encouraging and forward thinking. We believe that a person's past does *not* define their future. When we have open discussions with our children, we always try to leave the conversation with encouragement and a glimpse into a promising future (even if current circumstances don't seem all that promising). Encouragement, encouragement, encouragement! You must wrap your honesty in a blanket of encouragement.

4. Always tell your child the truth before you tell other people. Your child should never find something out about his or her past from someone other than you.

5. Do whatever brings dignity. Ask yourself, "Am I bringing dignity to our child through my words? Do my words encourage and uplift, or are they confusing, discouraging, or negative?" We know you can be discouraged, but you must pay close attention to the things you say in front of your kids. If you're frustrated, that's okay. Find someone other than your children to share with. Find a close friend who gets it and share openly. But with your children, focus on encouraging words.

57: How can I help our child process the hard parts of their story?

MIKE | On an unseasonably warm night in February last year, we sat on our front porch with our children gathered around. Our objective was to assemble a new wagon we had just bought for our new farm (yes, we bought a farm!). The excitement was palpable because this wagon would carry our kids' toys, pets, neighborhood friends, and a few of their odd inventions.

We laughed together as we tried to stay on track with the assembly directions. We stopped several times to locate critical parts of the wagon, but mostly we had fun on a rare opportunity to be outside in Indiana in the winter without dressing head to toe in thermals. The conversation bounced from topic to topic:

What kind of animals will we have on our new farm? Will everyone get their own room? What will the new school be like?

At one point we began talking about adoption (which is not an abnormal conversation since all our children have been adopted). Suddenly, without warning, one of our kids blurted out, "I don't give a sh— about my birth mom." Everyone froze. Our other kids glanced quickly at us to see our reaction. We motioned subtly for them to head inside as we sat down on the front steps next to our solemn child. We asked lovingly what was going on, and then we listened. We did the best we could to help him process.

So how do we help our children process these hard, deeply wounding parts of their story? Here's what we've learned to do:

1. Give permission. You must give your child permission to feel, express, and share openly their thoughts and deep feelings about their tremendous loss. When you and I have faced deep grieving moments in our lives, we process with friends and family. We must give our kiddos permission to do the same.

2. Be transparent and vulnerable. We must allow our children to share openly and not interrupt them or redirect them (yet). A dear friend of ours has been walking through this with her daughter. Recently their therapist told her to let her daughter share her story (the good, bad, and ugly) and to do nothing but listen to everything she shares. No response. No counter. Nothing.

This is a hard thing to do. Why? Because when she says, "I'm worthless," you want to jump in and say, "Oh no, sweetie, you are worth more than I could ever say!" When she says, "Nobody loves me. How could anyone love me?" you want to interrupt and tell her how much you love her. You need to let her share openly without interruption.

There will be a moment when you can say all these loving things in response to her broken heart, but she must be permitted to dump every emotion out first. Your constant presence and your willingness to listen will build her trust in you.

3. Be authentic. Please be real with your child. Don't shame them for their colorful language or display of emotion. Don't try to soften the blow to your own system. Just listen. As people of faith, we remember that Jesus doesn't respond with shock to human brokenness. Jesus allowed human beings to grieve deeply in their sorrow. He loved people in a radical way that threatened some religious leaders. He charged into the mess of human existence without flinching. Be silent, listen, learn, give permission, and allow your child to be free with their words and expression.

4. Be honest. Your child's hard storylines may be difficult for you to grasp. You deplore the hardships they've faced. Because of this, you may want to soften the blow by skirting around the truth when they ask. Do not do this. Don't eliminate details, thinking you're protecting their heart. They are going to find out sometime anyway, especially with access to the internet. Honest questions from your children deserve honest answers.

5. Be compassionate. Your compassion is an ointment in the wounds of your child. Your presence with them as they grieve slowly puts the broken pieces of their soul back together.

6. Remain open. Be open to having this conversation as much as your children want to, always, for as long as it takes. These hard storylines are embedded deep within them. The images, the memories, the fear, the trauma they've gone through may never go away. They may have to learn to live in spite of it, and that may mean they need to continue talking about it with you for a very long time. It can be exhausting, but your willingness to listen is critical.

There's a reason we use the word "journey" so often in our posts, on our podcast, and in classes we teach. Adoption is a journey, not a destination. Navigating the hard parts of your child's story with them is a journey. You may never arrive at a place where there is no more pain, no more grief or deep sorrow (for you or your child). Be ready and willing to walk this messy road for as long as it takes.

58: What should I do if our child talks publicly about their trauma?

KRISTIN | As children try to process trauma, they are likely to talk about it with people around them. They do not have the abstract, long-term thinking they need to make choices about who is a good person to talk to and what impact their story may have on others. A child who tells her kindergarten class about her sexual abuse isn't trying to harm the other students, but she may expose their minds to something they are not ready to handle. She should not be ashamed to tell her story, but she needs a safe outlet to process. Here are some suggestions for you:

1. Protect others. Explain to the child that when we have a hard story to tell, we need to make sure to protect the brains and hearts of those around us. Their story may be too heavy for a peer to carry. Their peers may not know about sex, drug abuse, or prison. They will learn about it from their parents when they get older.

2. Identify safe people. Who are the safe people in your child's life? Who knows their story and will protect them? The child should have a few safe people to talk to should he or she ever need to process a memory or a question. This can include Mom, Dad, Grandma, the counselor, or whatever combination of people you feel are safe to talk to. This should be a small group of people who are readily accessible to the child.

3. Choose a code word. Allow your child to pick out a code word to talk about the trauma he or she experienced. The child's safe people should know the code word. If the child uses the code word, the safe adult knows to talk with the child privately. For instance, when the child whispers the word, the safe adult could get down on the child's level so the child can whisper a question or a comment into the adult's ear. Sometimes this is all the child needs to do. Sometimes the conversation needs to go deeper then or at a later time.

4. Never shame. The child's story is not shameful, just private. Always remind the child that their story is their own and that it is no one's business but their own.

59: How much should I tell teachers about our child's trauma?

KRISTIN | We face this question with our own kids several times every year! Each time, we must reevaluate where our child is emotionally and how we can help them be successful at school. If we determine that the school needs to know about our child's past, we then must determine how much to share. Here are some guidelines we follow:

1. Privacy first. Our child's story belongs to them first. We should never share any detail that we don't have to share. Keep the story factual and do not allow for judgment or discussion about the specifics.

2. The fewer details, the better. No one needs to know the whole story except for your child. You can tell a teacher that your child experienced food insecurity or that the child missed a significant amount of school while in foster care. Don't tell more than necessary.

3. Some details matter. If your child experienced food insecurity and now hoards or steals food, the teacher will need to know. If your child is afraid to be touched, the teacher needs to know. If the child has an FASD, the school needs to know. Trauma can affect the child's success in all areas of life but won't necessarily limit success everywhere. Determine what details need to be shared.

4. Healing at home leads to success at school. Teachers may not understand the partnership between the school and home. This conversation is a must. The child's success at home will determine the success at school. The child's feelings of safety at school will carry over into the home environment. A well-rounded experience of support and safety will be healthiest for the child.

5. Safe, consistent language is crucial. Our son, who experienced food insecurity as a baby, discovered he could get extra snacks from his teachers in second grade. Instead of reinforcing his safety, the extra snacks reinforced his feeling of insecurity and his belief that moms and dads will not provide for their kids.

With the school and our son's teacher, we came up with consistent language that we all used around food. The teacher and school were able to support our family and our son by saying things like, "Your mom always packs you a good lunch. Can you show me what you have today?"

6. *Shared goals lead to success.* The goal is to raise a successful and healthy adult. When we partner with the school, we support one another in raising this child. When we work together, we can help our child understand the expectations at school, and the school can reinforce the trust and security we are building at home. Our child's teacher needs to know a little about the child's past in order to help move him or her toward the future.

60: What should I do if professionals disregard our child's prenatal exposure to drugs, alcohol, and trauma?

KRISTIN | The effects of prenatal exposure to drugs, alcohol, and trauma are still widely misunderstood. Because we cannot see our brains, it is often difficult for others to accept that damage has taken place. How can we help professionals address this?

1. *Initiate.* We must not assume that professionals are witnessing the behaviors, academic delays, social delays, or difficulty with attachment that we see at home. Remember that the professionals we work with see only a glimpse of who our children are. We must initiate the conversation. Have any diagnosis available and do not hesitate to explain how that diagnosis affects your child.

2. *Educate.* Share resources with the professionals you know. Create a simple explanation for what your child is dealing with and explain your child's diagnosis in simple terms. It's easy to forget that the professionals must remember many details about many vastly different things. Share insight into your child's prenatal exposure and how it is affecting the child every day.

3. *Stay in communication.* Your child's needs will change over time as will his or her reaction to the prenatal exposure. Stay in contact with the professionals you work with so they can be up to date on how your child is handling the prenatal exposure.

4. Think of the future. Prenatal exposure changes the way a brain forms. The more we know about prenatal exposure, the better we will be as doctors, teachers, counselors, and parents. We are helping our own children for the future as well as children these professionals will work with in the future.

5. Find someone else. If a professional will not take your child's prenatal exposure seriously, find one who will.

61: What should I do when our child hoards, lies, and steals?

KRISTIN | Our children are often labeled as bad kids, and their behaviors are described as manipulative, bad, destructive. Once we know the behavior is coming from a place of survival, it is easier to empathize. However, it doesn't make the behavior okay. Here are some things to remember when children use inappropriate survival skills to cope with their trauma:

1. Consequences don't always work. A child who is trying to survive isn't thinking about consequences. His brain is acting out of a need to stay alive. Before we give consequences, we must first get to the root of the behavior. Is the child stealing food out of fear of starvation? If so, the child may be unaware of the cause of his own behavior. We can start managing the behavior by first teaching the child to recognize where it comes from.

2. Trust is necessary to change the behavior. The child must be in a place of security to use the part of his or her brain that can make logical choices.

3. Structure is vital. A structured environment will help your child know what to expect. Regular dinner time, bedtime, and routine will help your child's brain settle and manage feelings of dysregulation.

4. Change requires time and patience. This will take time. When your child behaves out of their trauma, respond consistently over time.

5. Shame never helps. If the child steals, respond in a calm tone of voice and help them return the item and accept the consequence that comes naturally from stealing. Support your child and stand by them.

62: How should I respond if our child damages property?

MIKE | On a warm, sunny, late-summer afternoon, I loaded our then 13-year-old son into our car for a drive down to our city's public works department. This trip would not include sightseeing and lunch. In fact, we didn't speak a syllable to one another the entire drive. Our son wasn't very happy.

The previous day, we stood in our kitchen horrified as we learned that the day before, our son had picked up a half-empty can of spray paint and proceeded to paint symbols on the curb in an upscale neighborhood just behind our home. He fled when an elderly neighbor saw his artwork and yelled from across the cul-de-sac in his direction. Damage done. We received a phone call from a different neighbor who knew us.

As we stood rigid in our kitchen, everything in us wanted to lash out, scream at the top of our lungs, and demand answers: "What… were…you…thinking?" I could feel a knot forming in the back of my throat. I dreaded making a phone call to the Department of Public Works to confess what our son had done. I feared the gossip of neighbors who certainly knew who did it. I was seething. I knew I needed to respond calmly despite my growing frustration. I could see that our son was becoming anxious quickly as we sat him down to discuss it. Lecturing, scorning, shaming, or yelling would do absolutely nothing but escalate his anxiety into a full-blown meltdown.

Instead, I calmly explained that the next day we would drive to the public works office, apologize to the manager, and offer to repair the damage. Of course, he resisted. That opened the door for me to explain that the neighbors could call the police and report him for destruction of public property. He quickly weighed the two options and decided to apologize to the public works manager.

Here are some items that helped us deescalate the situation:

1. Remain calm and firm. You're parenting a child from a traumatic past—one whose brain has probably been altered or permanently damaged by the effects of abuse, or neglect, or losing their first family. Oftentimes they don't think clearly when it comes to choices, nor do they act with impulse control. You and I can't expect them to think logically. However, this is no excuse for choosing to destroy personal or private property. So how do you respond to your child if something like this happens?

When we react harshly, we escalate the behavior that our child is already displaying. They are reacting out of their anxiety. In order for them to make things right, they must first calm down. Every time we react harshly to our child's behavior, the behavior escalates—sometimes to a violent level. When we remain calm, we help our child calm down faster and address the original issue.

Calmness and firmness win the day. When we learned our son had vandalized a neighborhood sidewalk, we were horrified. But we didn't react emotionally. We responded with a tone that was calm. We stood firm by not allowing him to disrespect public property. We tend to be a trigger for our children. As we work to bond with each other, our heightened emotions can cause the other person's emotions to escalate.

2. Permit natural consequences. Your children will face natural consequences for their choices. Let this happen. In the real world, real bad choices have real consequences. You never want bad things to happen to your children, but you do want them to experience growth. Sometimes the way our children grow is through a natural consequence.

63: How should I respond when our child provokes other children?

KRISTIN | Our two youngest sons cannot be in the same room together. They cannot sit next to each other at the table. They will make life miserable if they are at the same birthday party or in the same

Sunday school classroom. Sometimes we feel like we are never going to have peace, but doing these things has helped:

1. Redirect the child who is provoking. When you see the child begin to push the other child emotionally, step in. First try to redirect if possible: "Hey, Johnny, tell me about what you did today on the playground."

Sometimes a simple subject change is all it takes. You may want to call the child who is doing the provoking into the same room with you: "Sarah, it's time for your chores. Come join me in the kitchen." This isn't a punishment—it's a redirection.

If it's effective, you can let the situation go. If you choose to talk with your child at this time, tell them specifically what you saw: "I just saw you stick out your tongue at your brother. That is disrespectful. In our home we treat others with respect. I love you, and I love your brother too. Please don't stick your tongue out at him again."

2. Provide a safe place for the child who is being provoked. Children should always have a place to go where they are completely safe. In our home, no one is allowed in another person's room. Period. Our two sons share a room with a dividing line down the middle, and they may not step into each other's spaces. If the child is being teased, they should always have this space to go to.

3. Allow consequences to result. If your child is doing this behavior at school, other children may not want to play with them. This is a *natural* consequence. If a natural consequence happens, allow your child to grieve and then support them as they learn a different way to do things.

A *logical* consequence may be something that you put in place: "I have a special treat for everyone who can use kind words at the dinner table tonight. If you use unkind words, you will not be able to participate."

4. Set up both children for success when possible. Talk about situations that trigger the behavior. Talk to the child who is being provoked about ways he or she can handle interactions with the other child. For instance, this child may be able to listen to music on headphones in the car or sit in a seat that is far away from the provoking child on a long car ride.

Then talk to the child who is doing the provoking. What are some ways they can make a kind choice about how to treat the other child? On a long car ride, they may be able to keep hands, feet, and eyes to themselves if they pack books, music, a cozy blanket, or a DVD player. Talk about how they should interact with one another and what they should do in a situation where they are likely to act inappropriately.

64: What should I do when our child acts out against our family pet?

KRISTIN | Animals often provide a safe place for our children to connect when they are unable to attach to caregivers. Animals can provide therapeutic support to a child just with their presence. But sometimes this nonverbal connection can lead to a child harming an animal or acting out the trauma on the animal.

Years ago, one of our foster children was pinching the dog until she yelped. When he thought no one was looking, he kicked the dog or grabbed her tail. He was preschool age at the time and was gentle with other people and seemed to understand the rules about being gentle with others (including the dog). The behavior continued.

When I alerted his counselor at his weekly appointment, she regarded me with a look of shock and fear. She told me this was a bad sign and might indicate something more serious in his future. I looked from the therapist to my sweet child and back again. Something told me that this wasn't a life sentence—this was a momentary behavior from a child who was desperately trying to communicate something. Others around me feared the worst and suggested we get rid of the dog. Mike and I felt there might be something more we could try at home before moving into catastrophic thinking about our son or giving up on our family's beloved pet.

We sat down with our son and asked him questions about who cares for him and how he knows they care for him. He said Mommy and Daddy. We asked him what things he needed to have to stay healthy. He said he needed food, water, a place to sleep, someone to play with, someone to read him a book, and someone to keep him safe. We asked him what things Spot needed to be healthy, and he told us the very same things. We asked if he would be interested in helping us keep Spot safe. He nodded in serious agreement.

For the next few weeks, he turned his attention to loving, gentle care for the dog. He brought the dog in the car with our permission. He made sure she had her leash on for walks and encouraged her to look both ways before crossing the street. Over the next few weeks, he opened up about his fears about his own safety. As he cared for the dog, he took pride in his ability to help keep her safe. This led to understanding and conversation about his own feelings of being unsafe.

If your child is harming a family pet, there are a few steps you can take:

1. *Keep the pet safe.* Separate the pet from the child. Do not allow the child to have any unsupervised contact with the pet.

2. *Talk to a therapist* who knows your child and understands childhood trauma.

3. *Do not panic.*

4. *Supervise all contact* if you and your therapist determine that some contact with the pet is permissible.

5. *Search for the cause.* Remember that the behavior likely comes from a place of trauma and that the child is using the behavior to communicate something.

6. *Communicate openly* with the child about his or her own trauma.

7. *Do not shame,* but keep the child from situations where he or she may be tempted to do harm.

65: How can I help our child establish healthy sleeping habits?

KRISTIN | "Mom, I need another drink of water." "Mom, I need to go to the bathroom." "Dad, my pajamas don't fit right." "Mom and Dad, will you pray with me, read to me, tuck me in, check under my bed…" We've all been there. Difficulty falling asleep is typical child-hood behavior from time to time. When bedtime just isn't happening, parents and children suffer the fallout from lack of sleep. So what can we do?

Bedtime won't just happen on its own. We need to be prepared. One of our sons goes to bed at 7:30 every night even though he's getting older. We maintain the bedtime because it takes him a while to settle down. We have discovered that he has trouble relaxing, so he takes a warm bath before bed whenever possible. We like to have him put lavender bubbles or a few drops of lavender oil in the tub. We tuck him in with a weighted blanket and rub his back. If he's in bed on time, we have time for a story or a song. He doesn't sleep with a nightlight and does really well with a blackout curtain over his window. These things work for my child, but what can you do about yours?

1. *Assess the situation.* Take a step back from the nightly drama and try to look at bedtime from a new perspective. What is happening before bedtime? What is the child eating or drinking? Is the child watching television, playing video games, jumping on the trampoline? Are there times the child sleeps well? What are the circumstances like when the child is able to rest?

2. *Make a plan and write it down.* Write down a few ideas you will use to create a new bedtime. If the child likes pressure, you may want to order a weighted blanket or pile blankets and pillows on top of the child's legs, arms, or back. If the child loves music, add a noise machine or speaker with volume control. Choose a few books that are soothing and rhythmic. Choose some things to put into the plan that are different from what you have been doing.

3. *Invite your child to participate.* Outside of bedtime, schedule some time to talk with your child about his or her trouble sleeping. See if he or she has some ideas about why that might be. They may have good insight into the problem.

One of my sons must sleep with a fan. He relaxes immediately when it's on but tosses and turns if he doesn't have it. Take your child's suggestions into consideration. Invite your child into the new plan you have for bedtime. Remember to keep the language positive. You may say, "I got some great new bubble bath for you. I think you are going to love it! It really helps me relax, and I think it may help you too."

4. Keep a routine. To the best of your ability, maintain the same structure each night. I'm a flexible person, and I'm grateful my kids don't need to do everything *exactly* the same, but we do keep the same structure. For instance, we always brush teeth, take a bath (even if it has to be a short one), tell or read a story, and pray together. We can do this routine in ten minutes if needed, but we keep it as consistent as possible.

5. Bedtime is not a punishment. Bedtime should be something you and your child look forward to. They should feel relaxed when they think about their favorite sheets, stuffed animals, books, and songs.

66: How can I relieve our child's anxiety at bedtime?

KRISTIN | Though the bedtime routine is important, it probably won't be a quick fix. Childhood trauma extends throughout life. Security takes a long time to build. Nighttime is especially difficult because the day slows down and there is time to think and process.

1. Be there for your child while they experience the trauma. You will do much to heal your child by simply being present. Your child may need extra time and attention at night. This is normal.

2. Set a boundary but also be flexible. For example, "You must stay in your room, but I will stay with you," or "You may start out in my room, but then I will move you to your room." "You cannot sleep with the light on, but I would love to take you to the store to pick out a special night light just for you." "We don't sleep with the television on at our house—I know you are used to that. I'll get you the DVD player. You can start out with a movie on, and I'll turn it off when I go to bed."

3. Find things that help the child relax. Here are a few things our children love: essential oils in a diffuser, a special nightlight, a weighted blanket, special jammies, and sleeping with Mom's or Dad's sweatshirt.

4. Acknowledge the anxiety. If the child is old enough to explain what's going on, listen. If not, you may need to hold him or her until they fall asleep, put a mattress beside the bed and sleep next to them, or even set up a place in your own room for them to sleep until they are feeling more comfortable.

67: What should I do if our child resists sleeping in his or her own room?

KRISTIN | One of our sons was 13 months old when he came to live with us. He had lived in a variety of places in his short life, most notably in a homeless shelter with his mom, sister, and approximately 100 other women and children. The first night he was home, I tucked him safely into his own crib in his very own quiet bedroom. I turned on the nightlight and closed the door behind me. Before I even released the doorknob, the wailing began. I'm not talking cries, I'm talking shrieks. Fear, despair, and loss creeped beneath the closed door with each fresh cry. I went back in and held him close. I spent that first night rocking him and whispering "shhhh." Mike and I tried everything we knew to get him to fall asleep that following week. Finally we moved our bed into his room, and though he didn't sleep through the night for years, he was able to settle back down with us nearby.

1. Set a boundary that you and the child can live with. Part of growing up is learning to live within structure. We must drive the speed limit, arrive at work on time, and get our work done. We learn these principles throughout our childhood and practice them with our parents. We also must learn that balance is vitally important as well. We may want our child to sleep soundly each night in his or her own bed, but this may not be possible. Make a boundary that both you and the child can embrace.

2. How important is it for the child to sleep in his or her own room? Can the child get a better night's sleep somewhere else? You may need to have the child sleep in a bed in your room for a while. You may need to sleep on a couch next to the child until he or she can settle into a better sleep routine. Can the child sleep in a room with a sibling? Would the child prefer to sleep in a tent set up in their own room? Remember that the desired outcome is healthy rest. You may have to take a detour in order to reach the goal.

3. *If their room is the best place, make it safe, secure, and welcoming.* Does the child need a fan or a sound machine? Do they need a different nightlight? Will a certain smell or a special blanket help? Is there something the child is afraid of in the room?

4. *Consider some compromises.* Some children have never had a specific place to sleep. This may be an entirely new concept for them, so you may need to compromise. You may tell the child, "We will sleep in our own rooms every night of the week, but on Friday, we can choose a special place for a slumber party, like the couch or a beanbag chair." This allows the child to feel like this is something special while encouraging them to get a complete night's sleep in their own bed every other night.

5. *Offer the child a transition object.* This could be Mommy's sweatshirt or Daddy's pillow.

68: How can I help a child sleep in our home for the first time?

KRISTIN | A sweet ten-year-old boy arrived late one night at our home, which was completely unfamiliar to him. I left church early that night in order to have time to swing by the Department of Child Services and pick him up as an emergency placement. We didn't have a room set up, so I made the couch as comfortable as possible and then awkwardly tucked him in. "What do you normally do at bedtime?" I asked. He launched into a list a mile long of things that would help him sleep. It made me smile despite the situation. "Oh, and I wet the bed…" he finished, quite satisfied with himself for telling me everything I needed to know. I stripped the bed I just made up and went in search of something that would protect my couch. I returned with a plastic tablecloth and completed as much of the bedtime schedule I could muster at that late hour.

Bedtime is hard for most kids, but when we have a new child come into our home, we must remember that bedtime is extra difficult for them. Bedtime is a quiet time of reflection. Fears and worries can be magnified in the darkness. We can support a new arrival to our home by doing a few important things:

1. Do research. If it is possible to ask the child or the child's previous caregiver for information about their bedtime routine, this should be your first step. Get a feel for what the child's expectations will be as well as some of the strengths you can draw from and weakness you can help improve over time.

2. Plan ahead. You may not be able to create an ideal environment for sleep right away. Try to set aside some time to create an environment for the child during the day. Plan your bedtime routine and make sure you have everything you need to help it run smoothly.

3. Be patient. It may take the child a very long time to relax at bedtime. That's okay. Stick with it.

4. Be flexible. If what you are doing doesn't work, change the plan.

69: How can I teach our child to relax at night without a bottle or other food?

KRISTIN | Food insecurity can be a struggle for all children, especially little ones. Small children may feel afraid of not having enough to eat but may be unable to express that fear. Children may also be used to using food as a coping mechanism. This is understandable, but it is not a healthy long-term plan for helping the child fall asleep. If a new child in your home is accustomed to going to bed with a bottle or other snack, here are a few steps you can take to help them break this habit:

1. Transition over time. Don't just take the food/bottle away. Start by watering down the bottle and eventually moving to water. If the child is used to having a snack, start with something very low calorie and gradually set limits on when and how much food is available at bedtime or during the night.

2. Be patient. Begin to move the food away from bedtime slowly. Having a snack before bedtime will help ease the transition. Then the child can brush their teeth, use the bathroom, and settle into the remainder of the bedtime routine.

70: How can I keep our sleepwalking child safe?

KRISTIN | Sleepwalking can be terrifying. Often a child who is sleepwalking will act out something that occurred during the day or something they have been thinking about doing. A child may try to walk the dog, use the bathroom, fix a snack, or even bake some cookies. Sometimes the sleepwalker will return to bed with no harm done, but the possible dangers are enough to keep any parent awake. If you have a child who is sleepwalking, here are a few things you can do:

1. Purchase window alarms. These are available at hardware stores. You can use a video monitor activated by movement or put a bell on the child's door to wake you up if there is movement.

2. Talk to your doctor. A professional may be able to offer steps you can take to help your child relax before bedtime to help maintain a full night's sleep.

3. Check with a therapist. If the sleepwalking persists, talk with your child's therapist to see if there may be any underlying cause that should be addressed.

71: When a child requires supervision 24 hours a day, how can I keep them safe and rest too?

KRISTIN | This is a question we get all the time. I can't stress enough that we have been there! One of our children needs supervision all the time. This child can't take a shower, pack lunch, jump on the trampoline, or even watch television without adult supervision. It is physically and emotionally exhausting to keep eyes on a child all the time. We found a few things that help:

1. Use baby monitors and door alarms. These are our saving grace in parenting children who need supervision. You can purchase these at any hardware store or department store.

2. Lock up dangerous items. This includes the pantry or knives. Have other children lock their rooms if needed. We use a large toolbox with a padlock for medications. We also have a closet that locks with a key for items that are tempting to our child.

3. You must have support. It can be frustrating, embarrassing, and isolating to have a child who must be watched at all times. Please know that you are not alone. It may take some time to find others who understand, but they are out there. Do your best to educate friends and family members on your child's needs. Not everyone will understand or be helpful, but when you find the right person, the relationship is priceless. Allow your support system to support you.

4. It's okay to take a break. When you do, prepare your child and your home so there are minimal or no disruptions.

72: How can I help children who have frequent nightmares?

KRISTIN | Bad dreams are a part of childhood. I had my fair share as a child. My poor mother came racing to my room more times than I can count because I was inconsolable over my very real fear that a giant earthworm was going to eat my family or some such thing. Children who have experienced trauma may be processing that trauma while they sleep, and nighttime can become a fearful time for them. It can be exhausting and frustrating to have a child who is struggling through nightmares. It is so important that we create an environment of felt safety around the child. We know that the dream was not real and that the child is safe, but they do not know or feel that safety.

1. Attend to the child. No, you are not spoiling a child by making him or her feel safe. You are helping them re-regulate. This is called co-regulation, and it is a vital step in learning self-regulation.

2. Practice patience. Take a few deep breaths, especially if this is the tenth time this week. Fix a place for your child to sleep on your floor, or sit with them while they fall back to sleep. It is frustrating to be awake in the middle of the night, but if you are able to be patient, you will help your child build a sense of security over time.

3. Make yourself comfortable. There is no need for you to lose a whole night's sleep over a disruption. Keep an extra blanket and pillow handy for yourself so you can comfortably sit beside your child while they fall back to sleep. Place small nightlights in the hallway so you do not have to turn on any lights if you need to get up in the middle of the night.

73: How can I help a child who wets the bed and then can't go back to sleep?

KRISTIN | Bedwetting is common and should not create a sense of shame or frustration. If your child is wetting the bed and can't fall back to sleep, help the child prepare ahead of time for what to do.

1. Use overnight underwear if possible. Some children wet through the protective underwear, and it ends up being a waste of money.

2. Use plastic sheets and easily removable blankets. Keep an extra set near the bed.

3. Teach your child what to do when he or she wets. Have a place for wet sheets and pajamas and a fresh set available and accessible before the child goes to bed.

4. Instead of sheets, consider using a folded blanket. This simplifies remaking the bed.

5. Remember to never shame.

6. Leave a small light on for the child so he doesn't wake up fully.

74: What should I do if my toddler wakes up at night and needs me there to fall back asleep?

KRISTIN | "You are going to spoil that baby!" I've heard that warning more times than I can count. Let me tell you two things:

(1) You cannot spoil a baby. (2) Ignore unsolicited advice.

When my own toddler needed me each night at bedtime, I felt concerned that I might be spoiling him. I trusted my gut and stayed with him until he felt safe. I'm so glad I did. He is not spoiled. In fact, at 15 years old, he sleeps quite well through the night. If your toddler needs you to help him or her fall asleep, here is what you can do:

1. Stay with them for as long as it takes. It will not be forever. If your child wakes up, you may need to start the bedtime routine over again in the middle of the night.

2. Help your child relax at bedtime. You may need to pat the child's back. Or you may need to rock the child. Find what works for the child and do it for as long as it takes for them to feel secure.

3. Try to remove yourself over time as the child begins to self-sooth. As the child feels secure, they may only need to hear your voice or feel you put a blanket on top of them.

75: What should I do if our child is daytime or nighttime wetting?

KRISTIN | Daytime or nighttime wetting isn't as uncommon as you might think. We have struggled with both in our home, at all different ages. Our urologist helped us understand a few things that eased our fears and helped us create a solution.

1. Is the wetting voluntary or involuntary? This is the million-dollar question. Let's first always assume that it's involuntary. When our children come from trauma, it's reasonable to attribute every behavior to the trauma they experienced. Diurnal enuresis, or daytime wetting, can be voluntary. But among children from all backgrounds, it's commonly completely involuntary. Let's always start with the assumption that the wetting is an accident.

2. *See a doctor first.* If your child is struggling with daytime or nighttime wetting, see a doctor first. They will be able to determine whether the wetting is due to a physical problem, such as a kidney infection, a urinary infection, or constipation. Your doctor will probably want you to remove certain things from your child's diet, limit liquids at certain times of the day, and practice voiding completely at timed intervals. Once every medical explanation has been explored, it's a good idea to consider other reasons the child may be wetting.

3. *Research emotional causes.* Document when the behavior is happening. Is there a certain time of day? Does it happen when the child is overly tired, anxious, or angry? If you see a pattern of emotional distress, now is a good time to see a counselor who is trained in trauma-informed care. If you are already seeing a counselor, wetting is something that should be on the counselor's radar from the beginning.

4. *Avoid shame.* Do not shame your child for wetting even if you feel it is being done on purpose. Shame never has the desired long-term result. Deal with the wetting calmly and matter-of-factly. Let your child know you see that he or she has wet their pants, and then encourage the child to create a solution to handle the mess.

5. *Remain neutral even when the behavior is frustrating.* Some children may not feel the wet clothes or bed sheets. Some may not care about the feeling. Do not shame but set a firm and calm boundary. The child must clean up after an accident of any kind. Use language with the child that lets them know you are helping them feel better: "Let's find some dry warm clothes for you. Here, I'll help you." Stay as neutral as possible by not giving the behavior more attention than necessary. This will serve to support the child while removing the possibility of the child manipulating you.

6. *Allow the child to be part of the solution.* Children should always be a part of the solution. If they are worried about wetting, they may be willing to wear a watch with a timer to remind them to go to the bathroom. They may take ownership in using tools that will help them remain dry. If they are not self-conscious about wetting, don't

panic. Remember to still include the child in finding a solution. Children as young as preschool age can learn to wash the soiled clothing. Choose a clean set of clothes and pack a pair of emergency clothes if necessary.

7. *Practice patience.* Whatever the reason for the wetting, it will pass. If the child is never physically able to remain dry (which is unlikely), it is still possible they will be able one day to manage the daily measures they need to take, such as wearing absorbent protective clothing, taking medication, or cleaning up after themselves. If your child is wetting as a response to trauma, remember that as you build trust and security for your child, the trauma reactions will fade.

76: What should I do if our child is hoarding food?

KRISTIN | Food hoarding is something we never thought we would encounter. We have plenty of food in our home. We eat meals regularly and have snacks available almost all the time. But for a child who has been hungry, hoarding food may be a behavior that is outside of the child's ability to reason. What can we do when we find that our child has been stashing a hoard of food in a bedroom, backpack, or other hidden location?

1. *Understand the behavior.* First we must understand that food insecurity changes the way our brains work. A child who experienced repeated hunger, consistent lack of food, or a caregiver who purposely withheld food will experience a shift in how the brain perceives hunger. Small hunger pangs become a reason to panic, and the child may move into survival mode. We must remember that the food hoarding is coming from the child's unspoken need to survive.

2. *Never shame.* This can be a difficult first step, especially if you find rotten food under your child's bed. Remind yourself of the reason for the food hoarding. If you find that your child is hoarding, don't panic or respond in a way that could cause shame.

3. Reassure security. Talk with the child openly about his or her relationship with food and reassure the child that they will always have plenty. Create a plan for the child to be able to see and feel the security. The child may need to always carry one snack in his backpack. A child may feel secure if she can always see into the cupboards or pantry. It may be helpful to allow the child to go grocery shopping and plan meals with you.

4. Set a boundary. Understanding the behavior is not the same thing as allowing it to continue. Letting food rot under the child's bed would be unsanitary and attract unwanted critters. Allow the child to have access to all the fruit or vegetables he wants—as long as the food stays in the kitchen. Allow the child to keep no more than one snack in her backpack at a time. Set a bowl next to the child's bed with one prepackaged snack inside of it. He may keep just that one snack there all the time. Use your creativity as you help your child set boundaries that reaffirm security while maintaining a healthy living environment.

5. Invite the child to help with the solution. Your child knows himself the best, even if he doesn't know that yet. Invite your child to understand the behavior and come up with solutions that will ease the sense of panic he feels around food.

6. Monitor diligently. Regularly monitor spots where the child tends to keep her hoard. Set a schedule, with reminders in your phone or on your calendar, for when you will check. Remember never to shame. If your child goes outside the boundary you have set, remind them calmly, "I know you are feeling nervous. I saw that you have five items of food in your backpack. You are only allowed to keep one item at a time. I'd love to have your help to get this cleaned out, and then you can choose an item to keep in there for tomorrow."

- Have you noticed that your child is struggling with food?
- What are some ways you can reassure your child and build security?

77: Why does our child seem lazy?

KRISTIN | Let's begin by asking ourselves a few more questions. When is this behavior happening? Is it when the child is doing a difficult or unappealing task? Does the child have energy for sports or playing with friends? Is the child sleeping excessively? Is the child able to do some tasks but not others? Is the child avoiding activities that would normally seem desirable?

"Lazy" is probably the wrong word. Children who were adopted are not lazy, period. When a child has experienced any type of trauma (such as losing their first family), the child's brain and body are hard at work processing the trauma. Healing from trauma is a tough job and takes a ton of effort. It is possible that a child may be mentally, emotionally, and physically exhausted.

If you are experiencing lazy behavior, it's important to dig deeper to find the root cause. When our daughter was 11, we noticed that she had become lethargic. She is naturally an introvert, so the change was subtle at first. She came home from school and climbed into bed immediately. She read books, wrote in her journal, and listened to music. Getting her to come to the dinner table was like pulling teeth. We eventually realized she hadn't had friends over or chosen to go outside in a long time. She seemed overwhelmingly sad. We were increasingly worried with each passing day.

We visited a pediatrician and came away with a prescription for an antidepressant and hope we would see a change quickly. We did not. On a follow-up visit, we expressed increased concern. Our daughter underwent a battery of tests. We discovered that she has a rare blood disorder and low levels of iron and vitamin D. The blood disorder would have gone undetected had we focused only on the "lazy" behavior.

The low vitamin D and low iron were remedied by adjusting our diet and purchasing the recommended dose of vitamins over the counter. We noticed a difference in her behavior within the week. Years later she can manage her own lethargy and depression by recognizing the symptoms and adjusting her lifestyle accordingly. Often behavior that seems lazy is really a medical condition or warning sign that the child is dealing with depression.

Our friend's daughter could have been described as lazy too. She refused to do chores but had plenty of energy to play with friends. Our friends were perplexed by the behavior: "We're asking her to do something simple, like sweep the kitchen, and she just stands there with arms folded, telling us it's too hard." When they dug deeper into their daughter's history, they found that she put up walls in many other areas too. She disagreed verbally with those around her about trivial things like what to watch on television or which vegetable is the worst. She refused to do any task that a caregiver gave, even things she would typically enjoy.

Her behavior wasn't laziness—it was really a coping mechanism she had learned to protect herself. She put up walls with people who might let her down, and she made sure she kept others out before they could reject her first. Our friends found a counselor who was trained in attachment therapy. Their bond with their daughter grew, her need for control lessened, and her capacity for everyday tasks like chores and homework grew as well.

One of our teen sons would constantly begin to do a task but never follow through to completion. He would pick up his laundry and carry it to his room but drop a sock, shorts, and two T-shirts along the way. Once arriving in his room, he would toss the clothes onto his unmade bed and begin building his long-forgotten Lego project. When we reminded him that he needed to do the entire task, he looked up with surprise at the pile of laundry on his bed. The room around him in disarray, he would begin to open drawers and closet doors. After an hour the room looked worse than when he started.

This same child likes order, but his room looks like it's been hit by a tornado. His personality and the behavior that looks like laziness are in stark contradiction. He is really dealing with an executive processing disorder. This inability to create a plan to complete a task and then follow through with that plan makes him frustrated. His frustration leads to anxiety, and his anxiety leads to avoidance. What once looked like lazy behavior is really the domino effect of a part of his brain that doesn't process information correctly. When we dig deeper with our children who are displaying something that looks like laziness, we will often find that something deeper is creating the behavior.

- Ask yourself, "What is causing this behavior?" Is the child overwhelmed, sleepy, or trying to gain control?

- Remember that this is a behavior, not an indication of the child's adult character, and it's a symptom of what is happening right now.

78: What can I do if our child doesn't seem to care about anything?

KRISTIN | Nothing. The end.

Just kidding—sort of.

When I was 12, my uncle tried to teach me all about the saxophone. He was passionate, enthusiastic, and informative. I was bored. He could do nothing to convince me the saxophone was the melodious piece of art he believed it was. I didn't care.

And that is the thing about caring. We can't make someone else care about the things we care about. We are all wired differently.

Let's identify what it is that we wish our children would care about and then decide whether it is possible. For instance, I value a clean room. If I leave my clothes on the dresser for more than an afternoon, they just bug me. I cannot crawl into bed until those items are placed in their proper drawer. I want our children to care about living in a tidy space just like I do, but for most of our children, this is simply not something that is on their radar. It is tempting to believe that the things we care about are universal values.

Let's look at this from my perspective. I care about a tidy space. Because I care about it, I think it's important. Because I think it's important, I believe that being tidy is the right way to live, and that leads me to believe it is the only way to live.

But now that I have identified what I care about, I need to ask myself whether it's possible for our child to care about tidiness. It may not be possible, and that's okay. If we discover that our child does not have the capacity to care about or value the thing we value, we can move on to the next step. We can set a standard of cleanliness that we can all feel comfortable with. Our children do not actually have to care about the tidiness of the home to hang up their backpacks and put away their shoes at the end of each day. Often, we are so focused on manipulating our children into feeling a certain way, we lose sight of the original objective.

Tidy houses are one thing, but what about caring for others? What about caring if the curling iron was left on, causing a fire risk? What about caring if someone trips over stray shoes on the stairs and breaks his neck? What about caring that it's Mom's birthday? It's a little easier to understand that our children may not care about some things we care about as adults, but we desire to see our children care for and about people and relationships. Here are some steps we can take:

1. *Determine where the behavior is coming from.* The child may look like they don't care, but their attitude may be coming from their survival instinct.

2. *Distinguish between perception and reality.* Our perception of a child's behavior is often different from its actual cause.

3. *Avoid making a feeling a nonnegotiable.* This is impossible anyway. You can require everyone to join the family dinner. You cannot require everyone to love and enjoy the family dinner. Don't try to require something that will just bring frustration to both of you.

4. *Respond with a plan.* Do not respond to the behavior out of anger. Make a plan and stick to it. Decide before dinner that everyone must sit at the table but do not engage with the child who is making a sour face. They have kept their end of the bargain, so maintain the peace. If making faces is your nonnegotiable, then require the child to sit at the table without making faces but do not require the child to love dinner or the meal you cooked.

5. *Don't try to make your child care.* You can't, so don't.

6. *Model caring behavior.* Tell your child how you feel about them or about others. Show gratitude for others and the things you have.

7. Don't modify what you are doing for one child. If you have a child who doesn't seem like they care, keep doing what you are doing. If you have a grown child who never comes to family dinner, Christmas morning, or family pictures, that's okay. Do not change your plans. Make sure to invite the child, be clear about the plans, and use words that help them know you want them there. Then proceed as planned with or without them.

8. Respond clearly and consistently. If the child acts in a way that is hurtful or negligent of others, decide what the consequence is and stick to it.

9. Avoid lengthy explanations. No amount of lecturing will turn the situation around. Stick with the boundaries you've set without the shame of a long explanation.

10. Practice patience. Be patient with your child and with yourself. Your best chance at raising a caring child is to show care for the child and for others around you, including yourself.

79: What should I do if our child lies about everything?

KRISTIN | "Did you take the cookie?"

The child shakes his head no while holding the cookie.

"Did you text the boy from school Dad and I asked you not to text?"

Teenager's eyes go wide as she swears on her life she didn't.

"Did you just hit your brother?"

The child denies the claim even as a red, hand-shaped welt forms on his brother's bare back.

"But I didn't get a C in math."

"I'm not drinking out of this cup" (that I'm holding in my hand).

"That's not my book bag. I know it has my name on it, but it's not mine."

People avoid getting in trouble at all costs. It's in our nature. When we have a consistent trusting relationship with the adults in our lives, we usually begin to determine which things are worth lying about. I stopped lying about cookies in elementary school, but I still fudged the truth as a teenager about where I was going with my friends. I grew out of that and matured into an adult who only occasionally lies to the stranger in the salon who is wondering if her new trendy haircut looks good. Lying isn't uncommon, but to children with traumatic pasts, the lying often makes no sense. Trying to have an everyday conversation with them can be disheartening and infuriating. Here are some ideas to try:

1. *To the best of your ability, take away the possibility of a lie.* Our post-adoption counselor gave us this advice when we were confronted with this issue years ago. I didn't want to heed her advice because I thought our children should just learn to tell the truth. It turns out that she was right.

Our child's misplaced fear of survival caused the lying. Once I learned that, I could see the lie differently. I began to change my question to a statement: "You are not in trouble. I'm not mad. I have your grade card in my hand, and I see that you got a C. I already talked to your teacher, and we are going to do some tutoring before school."

2. *Don't expect instant change.* When you phrase the statement in a matter of fact way, the child should feel safe and respond accordingly, right? Sorry, it doesn't change that fast. It will take time. If you tell your child you have their grade card in your hand, they may still respond by denying the grade or lying about turning in missing assignments. Here's where it gets tricky. Do not go down the winding road of analyzing your child's survival instinct. Stick to the facts, reassure, and stop the conversation if necessary until they can calmly talk about the facts.

3. *Consistently monitor your child.* If you know they are stealing from other children at school, take away the backpack and sew up pockets. Then check every day to see if they are doing the right thing. Do not ask them, "Did you steal?" Instead, tell them, "I found this Lego piece that I know doesn't belong to you. We will return it together tomorrow."

4. *Be gentle with yourself.* Your child's trauma response isn't about you. You are a good parent for helping them through it. If you fail at handling the lying properly, admit it and try again tomorrow. Extend yourself grace that you need to dust off and try again.

80: How should I handle an
older child's tantrum in public?

KRISTIN | I wish I could say this has never happened, but I would be lying. Our children who come from trauma are often functioning at a maturity level that is far below that of their peers. If repeated trauma, mental illness, or prenatal drug and alcohol exposure are involved, we have a recipe for teens who can't help but occasionally behave like toddlers. The problem with teenage meltdowns is that we get judgmental stares from onlookers. So what can we do when we know the tantrum is partly out of our child's control?

1. Set your child up for success. Prepare before you go anywhere. Do your best to let the child know exactly what is going to happen while you are out. Talk through what you will do if something changes. Practice coping skills at home so they are ready to use and fresh in the child's mind. Remember, this is not a time to shame the child—you are setting them up for success. Let your child know your expectations for the time you will be out.

If you have a child who sometimes needs to take a walk to cool off, this is okay, but let the child know what the boundary is in public. Can they walk out to the restaurant parking lot, or is it in an unsafe neighborhood? Can they take a walk to the bathroom instead if needed? Do your best to plan for the outing ahead of time.

2. If it happens anyway, ignore the onlookers. If your 17-year-old son is lying across the bench at the restaurant and refusing to eat, that's okay. Just go on with your meal. If your 16-year-old daughter yells at you in the store, walk away. If your 9-year-old has a meltdown at the state fair, calmly redirect him to a place where he can calm down. For a child who is smaller than you, place yourself in a nonthreatening stance. Put your palms on your knees so you can give your child your full attention at their level. Ask to see their eyes, but do not require your child to maintain eye contact. A simple connection during a public meltdown will go a long way. Ignore anyone who is watching the interaction with your child. They are not a part of your child's life—their opinion doesn't matter. In this moment, you are connecting with your child and teaching your child how to be calm.

3. Stay calm. I cannot stress this enough. Block out the feelings of embarrassment for now. Concentrate on your child.

4. Don't engage. Such a contradiction, right? We are working on connection, but sometimes our best move is not to engage. During the meltdown, our child's ability to reason evaporates. Do not engage with the behavior. Stay calm. Repeat the expectation calmly without engaging in the meltdown. For example, you can say, "I see that you are frustrated. We can't yell in the grocery store."

5. Always have an exit plan ready. Plan your exit before you go out. If you are out with other adults, make sure they know the plan too. If your child is old enough to understand, invite him into the plan as well. For example, "I know the state fair can be a little overwhelming. If you feel we need to leave, let me know and we will head straight to the car. If you are having a tantrum, we will walk straight to the car."

81: What should I do if our child is downloading pornography?

MIKE | Many of our kiddos have come from past situations that have left them extremely vulnerable to snares in this world. One big snare is pornography. Even reading that sentence probably fills you with anxiety. We understand.

What do you do when you've discovered that your child has been downloading pornography or viewing sexually charged or explicit material? Unfortunately, we have firsthand experience with this, and we've also learned through trial and error (mostly error) the best way to handle it. Here are some simple yet crucial steps:

1. Don't panic. When pornography suddenly invades your home, your computer, and your television, you may be shocked. It's critical that you don't show panic or freak out in front of your child. Keep your emotions in check when you are with your child—your child most likely already has heightened emotions over this. They may even feel deep shame.

2. Take action. Set up safeguards and put devices in one central location.

3. Seek help. Pornography is dangerous for anyone—especially youngsters, whose brains haven't fully developed yet. They're not equipped to handle what they're seeing. You need to find a therapist who understands sexuality as well as understands trauma.

4. Establish boundaries. Computers are no longer in bedrooms, phones are turned in every night before they go to bed and have no internet access, passwords are installed and changed frequently, the internet has a time lock on it, software blockers are installed on all devices, and so on. Write out your boundaries and expectations and post them.

5. Find community. Now that you've managed to keep your cool in front of your kids, you need a place to get your feelings out in the open. Find one or two friends who love your children no matter what and can listen to you freak out without freaking out themselves. We need that outlet. This is a difficult journey. Unfortunately, pornography is everywhere these days. Remember, it's not the end of the world. They are not defined by this mistake. They've messed up, but there is grace.

82: What should I do when my teen displays risky behavior?

KRISTIN | Growing up includes growing apart. I didn't understand this at first. When I held our first newborn daughter in my arms, I felt the enormity of the responsibility with which I had been entrusted. She curled her tiny fingers around just one of mine, and I felt like a giant. My heart swelled with love until it felt like it would burst. I vowed to never let her go. She needed me every moment of the day. Her bassinet was next to my bed, and I slept with one hand on her chest.

As she grew older, my love for her grew too. I curled my arms around her and pressed my face into her soft, curly hair. I checked on her throughout the night to wrap her blanket tighter or pop her pacifier back into her mouth.

Then something happened. She slept through the night. The first morning it happened, I woke to the sun rising and was filled with terror. I ran to her bed, and there she was, breathing softly, sleeping soundly. She hadn't needed me at all that night. Once I realized she was fine at night, the extra sleep felt glorious.

Then she started walking. Her tiny legs shook with hesitation, and off she went, away from me. I was filled with delight and wonder and fear. Keeping her safe became more difficult each day. Each time she tried something new, I fought back the desire to step in. This is natural, this growing apart. Our love for each other is no less than that first day I saw her face, but her need for me is different. This separation is good. But what do we do when natural pushing away becomes dangerous?

Regardless of our child's background, risky behavior is always a possibility. Testing the boundaries is normal and healthy, but when a child crosses the line—sneaks out, sets fires, obsesses about weapons, seeks out fights, engages in sexual behavior, steals, and so on—we need to step in. If our child's safety is in question, we need to take steps to keep them safe. Here's how to get started:

1. Define "safe behavior." You will need to tailor this conversation to your situation.

Safe behavior in the car is…

Safe behavior in a dating relationship is…

Safe behavior online is…

Decide beforehand what you are comfortable with and don't budge on the standard. Decide ahead of time what you can compromise on and then be open to listen to what your teen says. For example, consider driving. In our family, we do not permit our teen to drive with more than two friends in the car at a time. We insist on seat belts at all times, and we do not allow any phone usage. When we have this conversation with our teen, she agrees that she will lose the privilege of driving if she breaks any of these rules. Seat belts and undistracted driving are nonnegotiable. However, having three friends in the car may be permitted if the child negotiates the arrangement ahead of time.

2. Set firm boundaries. Continuing with the example of driving, safety in the car is a must, so wearing seat belts is a firm boundary. If we discover that our child is choosing not to wear a seat belt, driving privileges are removed immediately.

Moving from driving to internet usage…this can be a little bit tricky. Decide what the boundary is and then follow through. If your boundary is no phones in the bedroom, that means just that. There is no wiggle room because this is an issue of safety.

3. Use simple language and write it down. Keep rules simple and post them. When I first learned to drive, my parents posted my rules in the car. It was a little embarrassing to have them in plain sight on the dashboard for all my friends to see, but there was no denying that I knew the rules. Having my rules clearly defined also gave me an escape when my friends pushed me to do something risky. If my friends wanted to pile 20 peers into the car and joyride, I could simply point to the rules, roll my eyes, and say, "You know my dad…if he finds out, I'll lose the car for the rest of the semester." (As a side note, my friends did know my dad because he was their principal!)

4. Focus on safety. As our children create their own path, their values are likely to be different from ours. My parents didn't want me to get my ears double pierced because they felt uncomfortable with it, but it wasn't a safety issue. My parents also didn't want me to meet up with a group of kids in my neighborhood who liked to drag race. That *was* a safety issue. Drag racing is illegal and reckless. My parents were wise to separate the two issues. They let me know they would prefer I wait to get any piercings until I was an adult, but the final decision was up to me. They firmly forbade me to drag race—I had no choice in the matter.

Talk with your teen about risky and unsafe behavior. Your teen will want to do many things you don't like. Only a few things will be unsafe. Focus on safety and set firm, nonnegotiable boundaries around the things that are unsafe.

5. Allow some risk. I'm the kind of mom who sits up at night worrying long after everyone has fallen asleep. I think of the things that happened throughout the day and the ways they could have gone wrong. Then I anxiously think of ways that things could go wrong the next day. I see danger everywhere! I did that when our children were babies, and now that they are teenagers, I sense danger at every turn.

Our daughters recently wanted to go see a movie—a reasonable request for a 16- and 17-year-old. I sat them down and talked about what to do if the theater caught on fire, what to do if someone had a gun, and what to do if they needed to go to the bathroom. I reminded them not to talk to strangers, and by the time I finally took a breath… they were laughing. It is possible that our children could get hurt at the movie theater. It's possible that our children could get hurt on a bike ride or hanging out with friends or walking, running, or simply breathing. At some point, we must step back and allow them to take some risks. I did let them go to the movies with their friends. They had a great time and were safe. Not every risk is detrimental. In fact, kids learn independence by trying things on their own.

6. Praise safe behavior. After the movie theater incident, I had to praise our daughters. I told them, "Hey, I'm sorry I freaked out a little about you going to the movies tonight. I know you will not put yourself in harm's way, and I trust you to be aware of your surroundings and make safe decisions. Thank you for that." As I have relaxed a little with our children about normal, everyday risks, they have opened up to me about some of the bigger potential risks that are out there. By taking small risks, they are gaining confidence that will help them as they face larger decisions in the future, such as whether to use alcohol or drugs.

7. Seek help. Sometimes teens' risky behavior goes too far. Our children's brains are not fully developed, so they still need us to be present and aware of all online activity as well as face-to-face contact with friends. We still need to know where our children are and what they are doing. When a behavior is so risky that we cannot keep our children safe, we must seek help. Chatting online with strangers, sexually promiscuous behavior, substance abuse, sneaking out, and running away are just a few behaviors that can put a child in danger. Seek out counseling, rehabilitation, or even the help of the police if your child is incapable of keeping themselves and others safe.

83: Why is my teenager so angry with me?

KRISTIN | My sweet, precious angel suddenly thinks I'm completely stupid. We used to have a good relationship, but now I'm doubting everything I thought was true. She is angry with me all the time. She defies rules and boundaries. She argues over everything, and I do mean everything. If I say the sky is blue, she says the sky is light blue with white and gray clouds. I'm going to pull my hair out! She has threatened to drop out of school and move out, and she firmly believes that if she lived on her own, life would be grand. In the same breath that she pushes me away, she asks if I finished washing her favorite jeans, if I know where her lunch box is, and if I can fix her some toast for breakfast…Did I already say I'm going to pull my hair out? Where is all of this coming from?

1. Fear. Fear of growing up, fear of losing family, fear of having no support system, fear of being unprepared, fear of failure…the list goes on. Growing up is frightening. Teens are just starting to get a glimpse of the freedom they have longed for, and it is thrilling and terrifying. For kids with damaged attachment, this fear can manifest itself into an inner dialogue that tells them this family isn't going to stick around either. Teens can feel like they must prove their worth to the world and sometimes even their family.

2. Insecurity. Our son is afraid that if he leaves home, it might not be here when he gets back. When he finally admitted how he was feeling, our emotions were mixed. We felt relief because we knew what was causing the anxiety, but we also felt deep sadness for the almost-grown man who is afraid he will lose another mom and dad. Children who have lost their first family will often view everything through the lens of loss.

3. Triggers. "My birth mom already had two kids by the time she was my age," my senior in high school exclaimed one night over dinner. The thought just occurred to her. It's a fact, and we have never judged her background, but suddenly our daughter is processing where she has come from through the perspective of her birth mom. Things that might be fun for other teens—homecoming, prom, first part-time jobs—can all be triggers that cause our children to worry about the future.

4. Mental illness. Sometimes mental illness does not manifest itself until a child is older and nearing adulthood. If you suspect mental illness, get your child in to a professional and do an evaluation.

5. Growth. Remember, some of this is just the natural way of things. This is a child's way of separating from Mom and Dad. We are supposed to pull away from home and make our own way. Be firm, consistent, and forgiving with your child, and be kind to yourself. This too shall pass.

Part 6

A SAFETY PLAN

84: What is a safety plan and how can I create one?

MIKE | A safety plan is protocol for what to do when an unsafe situation arises. We know what to do if the house catches on fire. We wear seat belts when riding in the car. If you live in the Midwest like we do, you know what a tornado siren sounds like and what to do when you hear one.

If you're a foster parent who's been investigated or you are parenting children from hard places, you need a safety plan. Safety plans can ensure your family achieves maximum health and can help you avoid suspicion if you are investigated or accused of wrongdoing. We believe every foster or adoptive family should have a safety plan. When you parent children from trauma, you will encounter situations that require clear boundaries. It's critical that all members of the family feel safe at the home.

1. Gather what you need. Start with a sheet of paper, a pen, your spouse, and a close friend or therapist.

2. Identify the situation that might become unsafe. Let's say you have a child who is starting fires. Fires can be dangerous. Your first step is to identify that you are creating a safety plan around keeping the family safe from fire.

3. Don't panic. If you have identified the unsafe situation because someone has already been harmed, you may feel defeated. Take a deep breath. You are going to get through this. Remember that you have done your best up to this point—you simply didn't know what you know now.

4. Write out simple steps you will take when a dangerous situation arises.

For instance, if you have a child who rages, your first step may be to offer to help the child use a coping skill. Your second step may be to encourage the child to remove himself or herself from other children. Your third step may be to alert the other children to the safety plan. (You may add a code word here so the other children know what to do with very little explanation.) You may need to train your other children to call a family friend for help or even call 9-1-1 if needed.

5. *Gather your team.* Everyone who works with the child and may encounter the unsafe situation must know the safety plan. If your child is acting out sexually, you will need to alert the child's babysitter, teacher, and anyone who lives in your home. It is not necessarily a good idea to tell the neighbors or Girl Scout leader. Determine what situations your child will be in that you will not be able to control. If you only see your neighbor over the fence and your kids never play together, you can feel confident that this is not a person to include. If you attend your child's dance class with her and you are able to keep her in your sight at all times, there is no need to share her struggle.

6. *Practice.* Everyone must know the safety plan and be able to follow it with minimal direction. Your safety plan may include simple phrases, such as "Private parts are private." Your child should be able to recite a very simple set of instructions: "Only one person in the bathroom at a time, dress in private, one person per blanket, stay where Mom and Dad can see me at all times." Review the safety plan when there is not a crisis.

7. *Avoid shame.* We don't shame someone who wears a bike helmet to ride his bike, and we should not shame a child or family who follows a plan to keep everyone safe.

8. *Document.* Keep a spiral notebook documenting any unsafe behavior and how the behavior was handled. You may need this if you or your child are ever accused of unsafe behavior. Share this information with a trusted therapist who will guide you in redirecting the behavior.

You know your situation better than anyone, so your plan will be unique. Here are a few ideas that might be a part of your family's safety plan:

- Separate genders on separate floors (or in separate zones).
- Give children their own spaces that are off-limits to other children.
- Buy cheap alarms for doors to notify you of doors opening and closing.
- Post the plan on the wall so everyone can see it.
- Rearrange your house so children pass by you to get to another child.
- Install wireless camera systems that connect to your phone.
- Keep sharp objects and medications locked up.
- Buy a box that locks for anything that may be dangerous to the child.
- Only one person in the bathroom at a time.
- No playing behind closed doors.
- Change clothes in private.
- Children must stay in view of a trusted adult at all times.
- Choose a code word so other kids know when to use the safety plan.

85: How can our child follow their safety plan in public without embarrassment?

KRISTIN | A safety plan is a written protocol for preventing unsafe behaviors before they start. Sometimes the behaviors we are trying to prevent carry a stigma. Sexually maladaptive behaviors, severe aggression, violence, stealing, and hoarding are not socially acceptable even though they are common for children who have experienced trauma. Those who do not understand the effects of trauma may judge someone exhibiting these behaviors as a "bad kid." We want our children to be safe everywhere they go, but we also want to protect their privacy. This is the balance we must find when using the safety plan in public.

1. Decide who needs to know. Not everyone needs to know your child's story. Even the people who need to know parts of the story may not need to know all of it. Your child's teacher will need to know about the plan if it involves keeping an eye on the child at all times. The resource teacher and school counselor will need to know as well so they can support with an aide to watch the child. However, the janitor or lunchroom staff will not need to know the plan or why it is in place. If you are going to a playdate with a trusted friend, inform the friend of the safety plan and ask if they feel comfortable enforcing it. If the friend isn't someone you can trust with your child's information, it is best not to play at their house, or you can accompany the child on the outing.

2. Talk with your child beforehand. Our children may feel shame over their need for a safety plan. Reassure them that they should not feel ashamed. A safety plan is just like wearing a seat belt. We will probably not end up in a situation where we will need the seat belt. However, we always buckle it just in case. We will probably not find ourselves in a situation where we will have behaviors that are unsafe, but we always follow our safety plan just in case.

3. Create a special plan for public places. Have a separate plan that you use for birthday parties, playdates, the park, the grocery store, or school. Your plan should use the same familiar language but with situation-specific details. For instance, at home the child may be able to play in his or her room alone. In public that same child may need to be within eyesight of a trusted adult at all times. Go over the safety plan before you ever go out in public. Talking about the plan ahead of time will remind the child that they are not in trouble. Having a plan ahead of time will help the child not feel embarrassed if you need to call something to their attention.

4. Have a code word. Create a code word around the unsafe behavior. The child may not want others to know that his mom is keeping an eye on him, but if the child steps out of the line of sight, the mom or dad will need to call him back. Using a code word can help the child remain aware of the expectation without embarrassment. The word can be anything you choose. A phrase like "I'm thirsty, how about you?" or "Minnow" or "Honey, did you feed the fish today?" will not alert the others in the group that the child needs something. These phrases just sound conversational, like nicknames or cute inside jokes. Other people will ignore them, but they will alert the child that they have gone outside of the boundary of the safety plan.

5. *Create an ongoing plan for school, church, and sports if needed.* You probably do some activities regularly. You know the schedule and the people who will be involved at these places. Create a safety plan to use at the places you go to often.

6. *Praise your child for doing the right thing.* "I'm really proud of the way you played at the playground today. You were kind to other kids, and you stayed where I could see you the whole time. Great job." Point out the good things. Safety plans keep us safe. Yes, they are a response to an unsafe past behavior, but when a child follows the plan, he or she should feel proud of the accomplishment.

7. *Have an exit plan.* Always have a plan for how to leave public places, such as Thanksgiving dinner, the grocery store, the classroom, or a playdate. Plan how you will excuse yourself and your child if following the safety plan gets tough.

- Does your child have a safety plan?
- What are some ways you have helped your child in public?

86: What if our adult child cannot be independent?

MIKE | Parenting children from past trauma is tough for a lot of reasons. Many of us will be hands-on with our children for a long time, even well into their adult lives. A long time ago, I heard an old preacher talk about granting our kids responsibility when they grew older:

"We must arrive to the place in our parenting, and when our children are old enough, where we allow them to stand on their own two feet," he said.

That principle stayed with me well into my years as a parent. I knew that when our children grew up and became adults, we would grant them the freedom to make their own decisions and take responsibility for things that mattered to them.

Sometimes our adult children may seem to be incapable of making their own decisions. This is not a criticism but an observation. What happens when you allow an adult child to make their own choices, but because of limitations from a brain that's been altered by trauma, they suddenly begin to flounder? Do you stand by and watch this play out, or do you decide it's time to step in and make the wise choice for them?

I've been pondering this for a while now. Over the past decade, we've raised children who wanted freedom, even going as far as to tell us they can do things on their own and that we didn't need to step in. Most of the time, we graciously stepped to the side to let them choose. On several occasions we watched them flounder. It's heartbreaking.

It's like taking your child to a pool and hearing them say they can swim in the deep end, so you let them do it. For a moment they seem to be doing well. They are keeping their head above water, but barely. Pretty soon they grow tired. After a while, their entire face dips under and back up. They go from dog-paddling to exhaustion and finally they are in real danger.

As a good parent, you jump up, reach out to them, and tell them to take your hand because you're pulling them to the side. But instead of taking your hand, they say, "I'm okay—I've got this. I know what I'm doing!" Because of your lifetime of experience, you recognize that your child is about to drown.

What would you do in that instance? Regardless of what your child is telling you, you would jump in and save them immediately. You would be right to do so because regardless of your child's age, saving their life is more important than allowing them to exercise their freedom.

Now consider our children. Sadly, their past trauma has altered their brains, making them incapable of doing some things. Sometimes we need to protect them from themselves!

When do we step in and protect our children from themselves, and how can we help them succeed?

- Supporting a child who needs assistance is not enabling—it is critical to that child's success.

- Support is not doing everything—it is assistance so the child may successfully meet his or her own needs.

87: What can we do if our child is thinking about or has attempted suicide?

KRISTIN | According to the World Health Organization, approximately one million people die by suicide each year worldwide. Suicidal thoughts are not uncommon, but they are serious. If you suspect your child is thinking about suicide, you need to act.

1. *Create a safety plan.* Put it in writing and share it with every significant adult in the child's life.

2. *Include the child in the safety plan.* Let your child know how important they are to you. Empower them to take part in keeping themselves safe. Make sure they understand that you will be with them every step of the way.

3. *Lock up anything that could be hazardous to your child.*

4. *Remove the lock from the child's door if necessary.* When a person is going to harm themselves or someone else, they do not have the privilege of privacy. Your job is to keep them safe.

5. *Seek professional help.* Find a therapist who can work with your child.

6. *Take care of yourself.* You will need time away, and you will benefit from seeing a counselor of your own.

Part 7

SELF-CARE

88: What if I don't want to ask for help?

KRISTIN | Fine, then—don't.

Just kidding. Everyone needs help. Pride and fear can be barriers, but they shouldn't be.

When our children were little, I was a pastor's wife in every sense of the title. We spent weeknights at church until well after bedtime. We strived to have our children dressed and bathed with their hair combed and shoes tied every Sunday before the church doors opened. We loved our job and tried to be emotionally and spiritually present for those in our church community. Our role often left us vulnerable.

One day, a good friend offered to take our children for the weekend so Mike and I could go out of town. I made excuses for why we couldn't go. I protested that the children were too much work, and I worried that my youngest would have another asthma attack.

My friend calmly smiled and patiently waited for me to stop. Then she asked, "Would you watch our kids if we needed a weekend away?"

Without hesitation, I responded, "Yes, of course I would. I love your kids...oh, I see what you did there."

She laughed and asked, "Are you going to let me help you out?" I did. The kids had a fantastic weekend, and Mike and I were able to get some much-needed time together.

It's hard to ask for help. As foster and adoptive families, we have been met with misunderstandings about our lives and our children. Sometimes we have experienced interactions with people who did not protect our children, our family, or our story. We hear others gossip about our children's trauma responses, brushing them off as poor parenting or signs that our children lack character. But these people are not in our support group, and they are not close friends. When our children were young, I rejected help from everyone for fear of the wolf in sheep's clothing.

Turning away from all help is silly and leaves us feeling exhausted. I've been a parent for 16 years, and so far I have discovered that there is no prize for doing it alone. I've been waiting for a cookie or a party or something, and seriously—nothing. Conversely, there is no shame in raising our children surrounded by a tribe of people who love us. Asking for help is not a weakness, it is a strength.

So how do we go about asking for help?

1. *Identify your circles of support.* Think of the people you know. You have circles of people surrounding you. The larger the circle, the less intimate they are with you and your family.

- *The larger circle.* The moms and dads on the PTA seem nice, and they are fun to talk to at the monthly meeting. They know your name and recognize your kids. They would be fun to meet up with at the park for a playdate, but they may not be able to watch your child for you for an afternoon.

- *The medium circle.* The small group of friends you've made in your Bible study seem trustworthy, ask about your family, and seem genuinely interested. They like your kids and are likely to stop by with a casserole when a family member is sick. They don't know everything about your family, but they know a little of your struggles and joys. In this circle you may find a couple of people who can learn how to watch one or two of your kids for a few hours.

- *The small circle.* Your two closest friends were there the day your child came home. They have seen you in your pajamas, and they bring you donuts when a foster child goes home and you are too sad to eat breakfast. They love your kids through the hard parts and celebrate with you through their joys. These are the people you call when you are at your limit with a teenage attitude or when you need someone to pick up some of your kids while you run one to the emergency room.

2. *Interview.* It seems so formal, but choosing friends is even more important than choosing employees. As you choose who to include into your support system, ask questions. Decide what your values are and what you need from a good friend. Maybe it's knowledge of trauma, adoption, faith, integrity. Then ask yourself, "Have I ever heard this person gossip? How does this person interact with our children and family?" An interview doesn't have to happen all at once. Over time you will decide who can be in your closest circle.

3. *Educate.* Take time to educate those in your closest circle on how to be a support. Someone who will spend time with your children needs to know what their special needs are and what language your family uses. They will need to understand how you discipline and the structure you keep as a family.

4. *Pull away if necessary.* I have made more than a few mistakes in my life as a parent. I thought I could trust a person and later found out they were gossiping about our child or my family. When you discover you have made a mistake in your support system, pull away. Reset your boundaries and don't beat yourself up. You are doing your best.

5. *Share in the responsibilities.* When you build a support system of close people, participate in it. Don't be afraid to ask for help from these people. Don't hesitate to offer support to those in your group. Offer to host a playdate at your house, keep their kids for the weekend, and bring a cup of coffee to a hospital waiting room.

6. *Be specific.* Often our friends will offer to help with certain things, but even our closest friends are not mind readers. It is okay to ask a friend to pick your child up from school, bring a meal over, or baby-sit for an evening.

Asking for help is not a weakness, it is an incredible strength.

89: What are some simple
ways I can practice self-care?

KRISTIN | Have you ever been exhausted—*really* exhausted?

This is a book for parents—of course we are exhausted! A few years ago, I was traveling to see my parents. The drive was about four hours, and it had just started snowing. I'm from the Midwest, so a little snow didn't stop me. I loaded up my car with three of my youngest children and our family dog. After buckling everyone in, we took off.

My little ones hadn't been sleeping through the night, and the soothing sound of the car lulled them into a blessed slumber. And me too. Well, not quite. I stopped to get a cup of coffee. That helped for a bit but didn't quite do the trick. The snow was mesmerizing. Coffee didn't help, calling my sister to talk didn't help, singing along with the radio didn't help. I finally pulled over in the parking lot of a fast-food restaurant, locked the doors, and went to sleep. After 25 minutes I woke up refreshed. I drove the rest of the way without issue.

I needed rest. I needed self-care. If I hadn't stopped to take care of myself, I could have fallen asleep at the wheel, putting myself, our children, and other drivers at risk. Life is like this too. We must care for ourselves or we will not be able to care for others.

So what can we do? How can we care for ourselves? Here are a few ideas:

1. Take a time-out. A time-out isn't a cruise to the Bahamas, but it's a good place to begin. A one-minute time-out during a stressful conversation. A time-out when you are swamped with laundry. A time-out before you go in to another meeting with your child's principal. A time-out before you fight with your spouse. You can take a time-out by locking yourself in the bathroom for five minutes. You can take a short walk outside. You can take one minute to close your eyes and refocus.

2. Breathe. So often we forget to do this. Just breathe. When I was a runner (a long, long, long time ago), I used to burst with energy and adrenaline at the beginning of a race, but before long, my heart rate, steps, and breathing would even out. When we are raising children with trauma in their past, we can feel like the runner at the beginning of the race, all the time. It just isn't healthy to live like that. We have got to slow down and catch our breath. Pay attention to your breathing throughout the day. Fill your lungs to capacity and empty them completely. We can't always live in this state of calm breathing, but we can become aware of getting a healthy amount of oxygen into our bodies. We can take time to think about breathing while in the car or the grocery store line or while falling asleep at night.

3. Get help. Often we don't want to call out for help because it makes us feel weak. But asking for help is the opposite of being weak. As you find a good support group, it's okay to ask someone to watch the kids for an evening or pick them up from school one day. We have shared with our support system in a lot of creative ways. One adult we know is great at tutoring the kids in math. It's embarrassing how badly Mike and I stink at math! It's a sign of strength in our family when we reach out to our resources for help. About once a week, we get together with our friends and eat dinner. This is fun, but it is also a way to reach out for help. We each bring something to eat, or we pitch in and order a pizza. It's okay that it isn't gourmet. We practice healthy self-care when we allow others to help us meet our needs.

4. Eat healthy, rest fully, hydrate, exercise. Don't skip this paragraph because you are afraid of a guilt trip. I promise that's not where we're going. I love a donut more than the next guy, so I have no room to shame anyone about healthy eating. However, taking care of your body is good self-care, and good self-care helps you care for others well. Be aware of what you are eating and drinking. How many hours of sleep do you get? How often are you moving?

Now, what is one thing you can do better? This isn't a full-on life transformation—it's self-care. If you need to drink more water, find a water bottle you love. It isn't about punishment, it's about feeling better. You will feel better when you get plenty of water.

If you aren't sleeping well, spray your pillow with lavender, or find a blanket you love. Getting into your bed at night should be a treat, and sleeping well is a way to help your body grow stronger.

The same goes for exercise. I don't run anymore—I just don't like to. I do love to walk my dog, ride a bike, take care of my barn animals, and go for hikes with my kids. All these things are exercise, and they are all fun. Add something physical to your day that you enjoy doing.

5. *Take note of things that recharge you.* Are you the kind of person who likes to go into a dark room alone and sit in your pajamas while listening to music? Do you enjoy having friends over or talking on the phone? What fills you up? Set aside some time to do this thing. Parents often neglect the thing that recharges their spirit. Set aside time each day to do the thing that fills you up. Don't wait until you are depleted.

6. *Let go.* What are you doing that you don't need to do? Are you in debt? Are you working too much? Are you volunteering too much? What are your kids doing that isn't benefiting them or your family? It's okay to quit Scouting or choir or piano lessons. It's okay to volunteer for one field trip a year and not all of them. It's okay to duck behind your purse when the teacher asks for Parent–Teacher Organization volunteers. (That is purely an example, not something I have done.) Let some things go.

A few years ago, we bought an artificial Christmas tree instead of cutting one down. I thought at first that we had to go and cut one down because it was tradition and we had always done it that way. I thought Christmas would be ruined. Christmas was not ruined. We had a relaxing day putting the tree up, there was no mess, and the best part is, we can cut a tree another year. It's okay to let go of things that are jumbling your schedule and muddling up your time.

90: How can our kids practice self-care?

KRISTIN | Kids need self-care too.

Wait…isn't the whole world about kids? Why do they need extra self-care?

It is true that children are surrounded by things that are geared toward them. They are at school with desks made for them. They go to practices where coaches are paid to teach them. Play therapy—made just for kids. Kid-driven things are great, but they can tax our child's emotions. Our children need time to fill back up too. They need time to care for themselves in a way that will help them to be at their best as they face school, clubs, friends, and everything else life has to offer.

1. Time-out. This is typically a consequence, so maybe we should phrase it differently. Kids need a break from things too. They need some downtime between school and soccer practice. They need a minute during a heated argument to regroup. Kids need a little bit of time to think things over or compose their feelings, emotions, and words. A time-out doesn't always have to be a consequence. It can be a bath with extra bubbles. It can be 30 minutes watching a favorite show. Time-out can be 20 minutes of playing with Legos uninterrupted.

2. Re-regulate. Dysregulation is usually a lot easier to spot in a child than in an adult. Anxiety, sadness, frustration, disappointment, fear, anger, and overstimulation are often written all over their faces. Self-care for children is learning to re-regulate. Our children don't enjoy being out of control any more than we do. We can help them take care of themselves by first co-regulating with them—helping them regulate. Gradually they can begin taking the responsibility of regulation for themselves. When they have tools to help them regulate, they will be able to care for themselves well.

3. Coping skills. These are tools that your children will be able to use for life. The effective use of coping skills is a big part of self-care. Teach your children to be aware of their muscles, heart rate, and breathing and the effect emotions and feelings have on these things. Coping skills are ways to get emotions under control.

4. Friendships. Children need solid friends and time to cultivate these friendships. Our children may feel isolated by the unique structure of our families. Our kids need an outlet in friendships to share fears, joy, frustration, and celebrations. They need to build these relationships with a balance of guidance and freedom from parents. A child's greatest self-care can be with friends. Our children practice life through play. Our teenagers practice relationship skills they will need as an adult by navigating the ins and outs of friendships as teens. We can help our children practice self-care by encouraging solid, healthy friendships throughout their childhood.

5. Mentors. A mentor is an adult who invests in the life of our child.

Mentor relationships are a huge part of self-care for our children. As they interact with trusted adults, they can take ownership in seeking wisdom from others for themselves. Part of self-care is self-sufficiency. Self-care is the ability to meet our own needs. Having a mentor who is not Mom or Dad can help a child learn to one day provide for themselves.

6. Hobbies. Help your child cultivate a hobby. Each person was designed to function differently in this world. We each have gifts and talents to use. Using these unique traits brings joy. As you stand back and discover the things that your child enjoys, celebrate these things.

I have spent more time looking at car engines with my 11-year-old than I ever dreamed I would. I have attended dance competitions, admired Lego creations, and accepted gifts of carefully drawn superheroes. Each time I participate alongside our child in something that brings them joy, they are learning to use their talents. As they grow to use their talents well, they are learning also to care for themselves.

7. Identify how your child recharges. We all recharge our batteries differently. Our kids are the same way. Our ten-year-old loves to be alone in his perfectly tidy room. He reads books, draws pictures, and builds with Legos. I love to be with people. Sometimes I worry that I am disconnected from this child because he has spent the afternoon alone. This simply isn't true. By respecting his need to spend time alone, I am teaching him to care for his needs and care for himself well.

8. Remember the benefits of self-care for children. Our goal in raising children is for them to become adults. They will need to take over the responsibility of all self-care one day, including their mental health. If they have the skills when they are young, they are more likely to take care of themselves as adults. If they can take care of themselves, they will in turn be better able to care for others.

91: How can I care for my marriage?

KRISTIN | Parenting is tough. It is a 24-hour-a-day job, no matter what type of parent you are. Parenting children who have experienced trauma is an even greater responsibility. Remember that adoption itself is trauma, so this applies to you even if you have a typically developing child.

Our youngest gets in our bed every single night. Every. Single. Night. Our bedroom opens out into the family room. Mike and I sit there each night and talk, watch television, eat a snack, and just unwind. We never catch him making his way down the stairs, behind the couch, and into our bedroom. He has mad ninja skills. Sometime around midnight, we crawl into bed to find a very warm, pajama-clad nine-year-old hogging all our pillows. I have to admit, the scene is adorable, and I will miss it one day when he falls asleep in his own bed. If it's really late or if he's had a tough day, it is tempting to leave him there, curled up between us. On a rare occasion, we let him stay, but all other nights one of us scoops him up, carries him to his bed, and tucks him in. For now it is something he needs to do. It is a comfort in a world where he often feels sad, lonely, and frustrated.

Letting our child begin the night in our bed has not damaged our marriage. Letting him stay would. That child needs a little extra comfort each day, but he does not need all our attention. This is a balance I find difficult with all our children. When raising a child who has experienced trauma, parents must alter much of their parenting to accommodate the child. A child who rages needs help to calm. A child who struggles academically needs help advocating for his or her education. A child who often feels sad needs a compassionate listening ear.

Our marriages need that same careful consideration we give our children. Our children need a lot of extra care, but so do we. It is easy to see what our children need and provide for that need above all else. After a long day of school meetings, homework struggles, therapy sessions, special meal planning, mind-splitting arguments from teenagers, and so on, we need a place to decompress. We need time for one another.

Mike is my partner in this family. He is the reason we are the Berry family. He and I were here before these precious children, and we plan to be here after they are grown. If we do not care for ourselves, we won't be partners when the grandkids come to visit or when there are Thanksgiving dinners to prepare. We have discovered that guarding our marriage and our own space is vital to the success of our relationship.

Here are a few things we have found to help us stay on track and provide a solid foundation for our children:

1. Get a lock for the bedroom door. This seems obvious, but it must be emphasized. We have lived in two old farmhouses during our time as parents. Neither bedroom had a lock. This led our children to believe they were entitled to our personal space. I often do not want to lock the door because I think our children might need me in the middle of the night. Here's the crazy thing—they all have knuckles and can easily knock on the door. If you don't have a lock on your bedroom door, put one there. If you do have a lock, lock it.

2. Find someone qualified to care for your children. I understand how difficult this might be for you. I really do. You may have children who are dealing with past trauma, such as prenatal exposure to drugs and alcohol. You may have children who are in the delightful teen years. You may feel like no one understands our families, but this isn't true. It is worth the research to find someone to care for your children. These people can come from your natural support system of friends, neighbors, and family members. Seek out what you are looking for specifically and put the time into educating those who will help care for your children. Consider swapping with other adoptive families for a date night.

3. Trust that your children will be okay for a short time without you. I tend to empathize with our children's feelings of abandonment, so I'm reluctant to leave them. But when I trust that they will be okay without me, I strengthen their feelings of security.

4. Allot small chunks of time with your spouse. Time together can include a trip to the grocery store or a walk around the block. It can include sitting on the back porch watching the sunset. Time together can include sending the children to bed at a decent time and just enjoying the quiet of your family room.

5. Communicate with your spouse. It can be difficult to keep an open conversation with your spouse. Remember that you display a united front to the children, which creates a sense of security for the whole family. You must be intentional about this communication. Mike and I have been known to text each other in the same house so we can decide together (without the input of children) what we are having for dinner, what the consequence is for an unruly teenager, or where we hid the stash of cookies we hadn't planned on sharing with the kids.

6. Hold hands. I'm not an outwardly affectionate person. I never have been. It isn't in my nature to touch others for no reason. But I have become much more aware of the necessity of touch. When you are walking with your spouse, hold their hand. There are more words within one touch than we could ever speak to one another out loud.

How are you taking good care of your marriage?

92: How can my spouse and I handle disagreements?

KRISTIN | Mike and I disagree about a lot of things. We also agree a lot, and that is helpful when we come to a subject we just can't seem to agree on. We don't load the dishwasher the same way, and we don't make the bed the same way. We disagree about letting our daughter chew gum. We disagree about how to arrange the furniture. We have always had very distinct personalities and the drive to fight for what we believe is right. This can be a good quality, but it can also become tiresome in a marriage when the desire to fight is greater than the desire to cooperate.

When it comes to how we raise our children, Mike and I usually agree. When we disagree, we strive to find common ground. This common ground is worth finding and worth fighting for. I like to be right, but I absolutely hate being alone. I love finding a resolution to our disagreements so Mike and I can fight for what is right—together, as a family.

Here are a few helpful steps to conflict resolution:

1. Speak clearly. Choose your words carefully. As you communicate with your spouse, establish a topic and stick to it. A conversation about your child's curfew should not deteriorate into a dialogue about your pet peeves, such as the time your spouse left the toilet seat up. (Full disclosure: Mike never leaves the toilet seat up. Never.) If the subject is much larger, like how to address a child's aggressive behavior or how to create a safety plan, write down what you hope to accomplish and stick to the script. When you are confronting a hurt feeling or a miscommunication, stick to the incident in question and tell your side without assuming you know your spouse's side.

For example, Mike might say to me, "I told [child] he couldn't sleep in our bed tonight, but then you said he could start out there. I felt like you disrespected my boundary." When we communicate clearly, we can often find a resolution quickly and with less hurt feelings or confusion. I could respond, "I'm really sorry—I didn't realize you already told him he couldn't start out in our bed. I'll go move him now."

2. Listen without interruption. Why is this so hard? It just is. We all have an inner dialogue running through our minds. I've learned that I often think everyone knows my narrative and that they should discuss things with me accordingly. When Mike shares a concern, I frequently find myself wanting to blurt out the correct version (er...that is, my own version) of what happened. Don't do this. It won't kill you to allow your spouse to share his or her feelings, observations, and concerns. When we listen without interruption, we give our spouse the respect they deserve. We may even learn something we didn't know, and we set the stage to be heard when it's our turn to talk.

3. Talk privately. It's okay to talk in front of your children, the neighbors, or your in-laws about some things, but others should be saved for private discussion. Create space around the conversation and allow it to belong only to you. Come to a resolution in private and move forward as a team. It isn't a bad thing for our children to hear us talk about which way is the best way to load the dishwasher, but it may be detrimental to their security if they hear us fight about how often to have sex.

4. Set a time and place to talk about important items. Conversations about sex, discipline, the budget, and so on should be private. Take the time to find a place and time to talk. It's okay to say, "I'm really worried about how much we spent at the store last week. Can we get together tonight after the kids are in bed and go through our receipts?"

5. Keep an open mind, and don't be afraid to change your perspective. This goes hand in hand with listening. As it turns out, I am not always right about the way we should manage our finances. It is possible that where I envisioned the kitchen table is a hazard for my husband, who keeps running into its sharp edges at night on his trek to let the dog out. Keep an open mind on parenting decisions too. Your spouse may have a reason for doing or thinking certain things. When we listen with an open mind and an open heart, we can come up with solutions that honor us all.

- How are you handling disagreements in your marriage?
- Are you setting aside time to talk?
- What are some ways you could listen to your spouse better?
- What are some ways you could communicate more effectively?

93: How can we make the most of our date nights?

KRISTIN | Congratulations—you have all your ducks in a row and it's time for date night with your spouse. Yay for you! Pat yourself on the back because you are doing something that is healthy for you, your spouse, and your kids. Yes, when you and your spouse enjoy a date night, you are helping your kids too! Here are a few things to keep in mind:

1. It's okay to talk about the kids. We have heard many people suggest you never talk about the kids on your date night. I love the intent behind this suggestion, but the reality is that our family is a part of who we are as a couple. Mike and I kiss our little dolls goodbye, and before we reach the end of the driveway, we breathe in the freedom to be just us and to speak freely.

When our kids were small, we used to spell all the important stuff in front of them. I-C-E C-R-E-A-M after dinner? Our daughter was four when she began translating for everyone. (Have your little overachievers done that too?) Date night provides a time for us to talk without having to spell everything!

It's okay to talk about your kids, but don't make that the whole conversation. Set a boundary for yourselves before date night begins: "We will talk about the kids only while we're in the car" or "We need to talk about our daughter's college applications, but I also want to make sure we have time to talk about the project you've been working on."

2. Talk about your goals and dreams. Remember how you felt before you were married? I wanted to know everything about Mike, so I asked lots of questions and listened intently. I loved to hear about his family, what it was like growing up, and how he felt about the future. We sometimes forget that we don't know everything there is to know about our spouse. This is a great time to talk about what you still hope for in the future. It's on date night that we talk about where we want to live when the kids are grown or what we envision doing that we can't do now—traveling, serving at an orphanage, or running a small farm for profit. We've come up with some crazy ideas together, and that's what keeps our marriage bright and alive. I love to hear some of the ideas Mike comes up with. It reminds me that we still have so much more to know about each other.

3. Meet up with friends. I like date night to be romantic, and sometimes it is. But I'm not that romantic in real life, and the pressure is just too much. Don't get me wrong—dates alone with my husband are awesome. I love having time with just the two of us, but meeting up with like-minded friends is also good for the soul. If you don't have close friends, take the time to develop some. We talk often about interviewing people. The same applies to our own friends. Seek out other married couples. Reach out to people who are foster or adoptive families. Meet up for dinner and see if your friendship is a good fit. We have met some amazing people just by setting up a time for dinner. You have to eat anyway, so why not make some friends too?

4. Listen to each other. Make yourself listen without interruption. Your spouse may share an idea or a concern you are not on board with. Listen to the whole idea and then ask more questions. You will learn so much, and you will show love and respect for your spouse through listening. Later, as the conversation progresses, you will get to share your opinion or your own dreams. You may just find that the idea your spouse shared isn't as far-fetched as you first thought.

5. *Allow yourself to do something that isn't productive.* You may feel pressured to make date night spectacular. I'm a goal-oriented person, so I tend to create a task list for each area of my life, including relationships. First, we are going to connect. Second, we are going to talk about our dreams and goals. Third, we are going to make out in the back of the movie theater. (Oops—did I just write that?) It's okay to go on a date night without a task list involved. Go see a funny movie just for the sake of laughter. Play mini golf just because. Do something fun just because you want to.

6. *Answer your phone if you need to.* I can't relax if our children (or the people watching them) can't reach me. It's okay to answer a call and explain how to boil an egg. It's okay to FaceTime your youngest and remind him he is to listen to his sister and get in bed right now. Don't let this take up your entire night out. Allow your kids and sitter to check in with you, but don't allow them to control your night. Which leads us to the last idea...

7. *Set boundaries with your kids ahead of time.* Talk with your kids about why you are going out. It's good for children to hear that Mom and Dad are also husband and wife. Explain to them that you will be available if they need you but that you will not be able to answer the phone to solve sibling arguments or to help them find their favorite T-shirt. Tell your kids the schedule of your night. Our kids who deal with past trauma may feel insecure about being left at home. It's okay to tell them what you will be doing and when you will not be able to answer your phone.

- When was the last time you had a date night?
- When are you planning a date night?
- What do you need to do to get things settled at home so you can relax while you're out?

Have fun...and happy dating!

Part 8

ADOPTEE PERSPECTIVES

Honestly Adoption is written by parents, for parents. We have written this book with the most important people in mind—our children. We have learned so much from our own children, friends who have been adopted, and adult adoptees in our community. We are grateful for how the adoptee community continues to help us widen our perspectives and sharpen our parenting skills. In this final part of the book, we asked our readers what questions they have for adoptees. We have truly saved the best for last!

94: Do you have a relationship with your biological family?

KATHERINE RACHEL, AGE 32 | Yes, I do. I am blessed to have a good relationship with both my adoptive and biological families. I think sometimes it confuses people because I don't run around referring to them as my biological or adopted family. But I don't think of them like that. They are all just my family.

I am probably more timid about my feelings with my bio family than with my adoptive family. There are many things I really don't want to revisit with them. It's a little different for me due to the details of my adoption. My biological family didn't really have much to do with that decision—I'm not even sure if they all know I'm legally adopted. Depends on who within my biological family I'm talking to. But still... I'm not super open with my feelings in general. If they asked, I would discuss with them. But there are some things I don't feel the need to share.

SAM, AGE 9 | Not really, but I visit now and then. I still ask about them, and sometimes I have dinner with my dad. It's like once a year, but that's all I need right now. I sometimes lie in bed and wonder what they are dreaming about. I mostly worry about their lives. Sometimes I feel scared to talk to my birth parents. I think they might not take me seriously. They might think I'm silly or that I'm just joking around. I haven't seen my birth mom since I was a baby. I might be able to talk to my dad—I think I could ask him any question.

JAKE, AGE 10 | I have a relationship with my brother because we were adopted in the same family. I also know my grandparents and great aunts and second cousins. I like knowing them because they are fun and they have good food. I sometimes visit my dad. Sometimes I'm afraid to talk to my birth family because maybe they won't want to talk to me. I can talk to Mamela (Italian for "Grandma") and Grandma Missy.

JAALA, AGE 16 | I have had the privilege of meeting my birth mother, but we have not kept up with our visits.

ELI, AGE 11 | Sometimes when I go to my grandma's house, my birth dad brings us McDonald's. I know my biological grandma and grandpa. I also know some aunts and uncles. I also know Jake, my brother.

HENRY, AGE 14 | I see my mom sometimes. She comes to my baseball games, and sometimes we meet up at Pizza King. It would be hard to tell my birth mom how I feel because I barely know her. I haven't lived with her for ten years. I think she would be surprised by how I feel.

I know my brother because he lives with me. We were adopted by the same family. Sometimes I'm frustrated with him, and sometimes we get along together. If we had not been adopted together I would feel worse because he's my brother and I'm supposed to look after him. I never really knew my dad.

ELISA, AGE 14 | No. I know who my birth mom is, but I don't really talk to her. I would be kind of afraid because I wouldn't want her to take what I'm saying the wrong way and not want to talk to me ever again. But I do want her to know how I feel and how everything affected me.

NOELLE, AGE 17 | Once in a while, I talk to my birth mom. I'm pretty okay with my relationship with her. If it was to be closer, that would be nice, but I don't need it to be. I don't ever talk to my biological dad. I never had a relationship with him. I'm not afraid to talk to them. I don't have any bad feelings toward them, but I guess I would be afraid to ask my birth mom something about the details of my childhood. I'm afraid I'll find out that she doesn't know or doesn't remember.

I'm afraid to ask her what time of day I was born because I'm afraid she doesn't know.

I live with my biological brother. Even though we were adopted together, I have less of a relationship with him than I do with my two biological sisters who live with other families. I haven't talked to my youngest (ten-year-old) sister lately, but I picked up my other (thirteen-year-old) sister to hang out the other day. I contacted one of my older biological sisters a few months ago, but she ignored me. I'm glad I know who she is and what she looks like. I wanted to know what her hobbies are.

AUSTIN, AGE 11 | I don't even want to think about my dad. I don't like what he did to my mom. My dad is in and out of jail. My parents did things that hurt me. I think they are divorced now. I know my brother Henry. He lives in the same family as me. I know my birth mom. That's all I know. I do miss my birth dad, but not as much as I miss my birth mom.

CHRYSTAL, AGE 8 | I don't talk to anyone in my birth family. On holidays I wonder what I would do with my biological family if I lived with them. When I look at a picture of my mom, I miss her. If I said I was hurt or mad, I feel like my birth mom would get really mad at me.

95: Do you celebrate your adoption day?

JAALA, AGE 16 | No, but I know that other people do. It's just not really something we do in our family.

SAM, AGE 9 | Sometimes remembering my adoption is hard because I was taken away from my parents. I was in foster care. I don't celebrate my adoption day, but I want to. I was adopted when I was three and a half years old. I remember a judge and getting candy. Adoption day is kind of like a birthday…I would like cake and presents.

JAKE, AGE 10 | Thinking about my adoption day makes me feel new. I came to live with my family when I was 11 months old. I was adopted a few years later. I remember getting a sucker at the courthouse. We don't celebrate the day of our adoption. I don't really care if we celebrate because we are family now. If we did celebrate, I would like to have cake and presents and watch movies.

ELI, AGE 11 | I don't think about the day I was adopted. I was adopted when I was four years old, but I don't remember it. I don't celebrate the anniversary. There isn't anything I would like to do on the anniversary of my adoption. Maybe I would like for my parents to take me to look at cars at a Ford car dealership.

KATHERINE RACHEL, AGE 32 | It's a happy/sad day for me. Mostly happy. I don't buy a cake or balloons or anything like that—not really my style. It's equally celebration and mourning for me. Don't get me wrong—I'm in no way sad that I was adopted. But there is a certain sense of loss associated with my biological parents, and that kind of puts a damper on celebration.

Ideas for celebrating…hmm…you know, just telling an adopted child that you are so happy that they are in your life. I think adopted kids know this, but it never hurts to hear it one more time.

AUSTIN, AGE 11 | I feel okay about my adoption day. It makes me feel happy and sad. I feel happy because I love everybody in my family, and I feel sad because I miss my birth mom. On my adoption anniversary, I would like to see my birth mom and spend the whole day with her.

HENRY, AGE 14 | When I think about my adoption day, I feel mostly happy but a little bit sad. I feel happy because I have a better home than I used to. I feel sad because I miss my birth mom. I don't celebrate my adoption day every year. I would tell someone to celebrate by meeting up with the child's birth parents or talking on the phone with them. If they are not available, you could watch a family movie together. I like to watch *Pete's Dragon*.

ELISA, AGE 14 | I have mixed emotions. I feel happy and sad at the same time. I don't like to think about it because it's a sad day for me. I wouldn't throw a big party, but I would like something small like a necklace to remember the day.

NOELLE, AGE 17 | Honestly, I don't even know what day I was adopted. I know I was six. I think it would have a bigger impact on me if I had lived with my birth mom longer. I was three when I lived with her. The transition to my new family wasn't as hard as I think it would have been for my older sister, who was fifteen.

CHRYSTAL, AGE 8 | I was adopted when I was seven years old. Sometimes I feel happy, but sometimes I feel like if I hadn't been adopted, I would be with my birth family. I know that isn't true because I was in foster care. I wish the world was rainbows and cupcakes.

96: How can a family help a new child feel welcome?

SAM, AGE 9 | I came to live with my family when I was three days old. I don't remember what it was like. If a new child comes into your home, you should talk softly around them, make sure they have something of their own, make sure the other kids are sharing, and tell them they are welcome always and forever.

JAALA, AGE 16 | Just by giving them the space they need to adjust, but also letting them know that they are there for them to talk to.

JAKE, AGE 10 | I don't remember coming to my home. If you are bringing a new child home, you should help them meet new friends.

KATHERINE RACHEL, AGE 32 | Let them pick what's for dinner. Give them some things of their own—toiletries and other small items... maybe something meaningful to your family (especially something they can do with the family). Kids like feelings of belonging and having belongings.

HENRY, AGE 14 | I don't remember coming into my new home. I was four years old. If you are bringing a new child into your home, you should support them in any way you can. You should introduce them to everyone in the home. You should tell them you are happy to have them in your home.

AUSTIN, AGE 11 | I don't remember coming into my new family because I was young. All I remember is that my birth mom was hurt by my birth dad. If you are bringing a new child home, you could buy them a present, give them their own room, and maybe take them someplace fun to get their mind off things. You could meet their birth mom. It's good for you to know their birth mom. The child might miss their birth mom, and he or she might want to see her. The child might have been in foster care in a lot of homes, trying to find the right family.

CHRYSTAL, AGE 8 | I remember feeling happy because I had a family to live with instead of being in foster care. If someone brings a new child home, they should take care of them. You could give them a day off from doing homework or a week off from doing chores.

ELISA, AGE 14 | I don't remember coming to my new home. I was a baby. If someone brings a little child home, they can give them a new stuffed animal. If they bring a teenager home, they can give them their own space so they can be alone and not be bothered by people.

NOELLE, AGE 17 | I don't remember coming to my new family. I was three years old. If someone was bringing a child home, the family should begin by trying not to make it overwhelming.

97: Do you feel like you can talk with your adoptive family about your emotions?

SAM, AGE 9 | I am not afraid to talk to my family because they are always there for me. Even in the hardest times, like when I'm a pill. Sometimes I'm really mad, and my parents curl me up in a ball and let me get in their bed and maybe read me a book.

JAKE, AGE 10 | I want my mom and dad to ask how I'm doing. I don't really want to talk about girls or feelings. My feelings are my business, and I can probably handle it. Sometimes I talk to my mom and dad when I'm feeling sad. They talk to me alone so no one knows what we are talking about.

ELI, AGE 11 | I'm not afraid to talk with my family. They are the only people I can trust.

KATHERINE RACHEL, AGE 32 | I'm not afraid to talk with my family, but I have always been more of a private person. I typically keep a lot of feelings to myself—I cannot ever remember not being this way. I suppose it depends on the subject as well, but if I want to talk about something, there is zero fear for me in discussing anything with my adoptive family. In regards to my adoption, there is nothing I cannot or would not discuss with my adoptive family. My parents know about my decision to ask them to adopt me—they know my heart in that decision. I don't feel any need to discuss that type of thing.

JAALA, AGE 16 | Yes. To me they are not my adoptive family, they are just my family.

AUSTIN, AGE 11 | Sometimes I'm nervous and scared to talk about my feelings and how much I miss my mom. I'm scared to see my dad. My adoptive parents like to talk to me about my feelings and ask me how I feel about being adopted. I feel safe talking to them when we are alone because I don't want anyone else to hear how I feel. I only want my brother around because he's from my birth mom too.

HENRY, AGE 14 | I talk to my parents anywhere. I feel worried to tell them that I want to see my birth dad because I think they might say no because he's not a good person. I remember when he hurt my mom. I still want to see him anyway.

ELISA, AGE 14 | I can talk about my adoption and my biological family, but sometimes I get scared to tell my mom certain things about my feelings because I think she may take it the wrong way. I think she will worry. Sometimes I just want to feel sad, but my mom says, "You need to come out of your room." My mom and dad ask me a lot of questions. I sometimes like to be alone because I want to work it out on my own.

NOELLE, AGE 17 | Sometimes I feel like I don't say things the right way or my parents will think I'm rude or whatever when I talk about my feelings. I feel like I can talk openly about adoption but not always about other things. I prefer to process by myself. If I'm feeling like I want to talk, I will. If I don't feel it's necessary, I won't talk about it. If my parents never talked about my birth family, I wouldn't know a lot of stuff about my (birth) mom. I have compassion for my (birth) mom because we talk about her.

CHRYSTAL, AGE 8 | I can tell them almost anything. I'm scared that they might get mad at me if I ask to see a picture of my birth mom all the time, like every day. If I asked my adoptive mom every single day, she might get mad and say no. Sometimes I want to be asked about my adoption. I want them to talk to me about the things they know about my (bio) parents. I want to know why my mom couldn't take care of me.

98: Do you want your adoptive family to ask questions about your birth family and adoption?

SAM, AGE 9 | Yes, yes, yes, very much. I wish they would ask every single morning, "How are you? Are you feeling good today?"

JAKE, AGE 10 | I want my mom and dad to ask how I'm doing. I don't really want to talk about girls or feelings.

NOELLE, AGE 17 | I've been able to process by myself. If I'm feeling like I want to talk, I will. If I don't feel it's necessary, I won't talk about it. If my parents never talked about my birth family, I wouldn't know a lot of stuff about my (birth) mom. I have compassion for my (birth) mom because we talk about her.

ELISA, AGE 14 | Sometimes I just want to feel sad, but my mom says, "You need to come out of your room." My mom and dad ask me a lot of questions. I sometimes like to be alone because I want to work it out on my own.

CHRYSTAL, AGE 8 | Sometimes I want to be asked about my adoption. I want them to talk to me about the things they know about my (bio) parents. I want to know why my mom couldn't take care of me.

KATHERINE RACHEL, AGE 32 | My parents know about my decision to ask them to adopt me—they know my heart in that decision. I don't feel any need to discuss that type of thing.

99: What do you wish people would stop saying about adoption?

JAALA, AGE 16 | "So who are your real parents?" That annoys me.

SAM, AGE 9 | That adoption is kidnapping. Sometimes parents can't raise their kids, so they need someone to take care of them, like if the parents are in jail.

JAKE, AGE 10 | I've never heard any questions or comments about adoption.

CHRYSTAL, AGE 8 | It bothers me when people don't know what adoption is.

ELISA, AGE 14 | I wish people would stop thinking adoption is a bad thing. If your family is abusing you, it would be better to live somewhere safe.

NOELLE, AGE 17 | Adoption is made out to be the second choice, like the family couldn't have biological kids and chose adoption second. This isn't always the case.

I wish people would stop saying "real family," "real parents," "real siblings." It's not like my adoptive family is fake.

HENRY, AGE 14 | I hate when people ask me if I'm adopted. I don't know how they know—maybe they heard a rumor.

KATHERINE RACHEL, AGE 32 | I wish people wouldn't refer to "real" parents or children. I wish they wouldn't say, "You can't love an adopted child like you can 'your own.'"

100: What should adoptive parents do when others talk about adoption inappropriately?

JAKE, AGE 10 | I want them to stand up for me and tell them the right thing to say.

NOELLE, AGE 17 | If someone says "real kids," I would want my parents to say, "They are all my real kids." Usually I will advocate for myself. If something makes me feel uncomfortable, I will address it myself.

SAM, AGE 9 | I wish my parents would say, "That's not true. How would you feel if someone said that to you?"

ELISA, AGE 14 | If somebody asks my parents if I'm their child, I want them to just say yes.

CHRYSTAL, AGE 8 | If someone asks, "What did your (bio) parents do?" I would want my parents to say, "That's none of your business."

KATHERINE RACHEL, AGE 32 | My family typically corrects someone by using better terms and such. Some people don't realize they are saying something wrong. If someone is intentionally saying something to be hateful, I hope my parents call them out, just as I would.

JAALA, AGE 16 | Correct them but not make them feel bad.

JUSTIN, AGE 11 | Someone at school said something mean about my family. They said, "That's why your parents didn't want you." I asked my mom to call the school or call the kid's parents. She did. That made me feel better.

101: Did your name change when you were adopted?

CHRYSTAL, AGE 8 | Yes, my middle name and my last name. When I was adopted, my mom and dad picked out my name. I feel good about my name.

ELISA, AGE 14 | My last name was changed. My birth mom and my parents chose my name together. I love my name because it's very unique. I especially like my middle name because it's my mom's maiden name and my grandfather's last name.

JAKE, AGE 10 | Yes. I feel proud of my name.

NOELLE, AGE 17 | Yes, I got two middle names when I was adopted. My mom and dad chose Noelle because I was born on Christmas and Christine after my aunt. My birth mom chose Carmen after the TV show *Where in the World Is Carmen Sandiego?* I have mixed emotions about my first name, Carmen. I don't want to put it down because it's the name my birth mom gave me, but I just like Noelle better. I think Carmen is a pretty name, but I like Noelle better because it sounds soft and Carmen sounds hard.

JAALA, AGE 16 | No. My (adoptive) mom and dad named me.

SAM, AGE 9 | Yes, it did. I like my name. Sometimes I want to be called by the name I had when I was born, but mostly I want to be called Sam.

KATHERINE RACHEL, AGE 32 | Yes, it did. I chose it. I still like it. It is meaningful to me and special. Not everyone can say they picked their name.

About the Authors

Mike and Kristin Berry are adoptive parents and former foster parents. They are cocreators of the award-winning blog *confessionsofanadoptiveparent.com*, which has more than 100,000 followers monthly and was named number 3 in the Top 100 Foster Blogs on the Planet in 2017 by Feedspot. It was also named one of the Top Adoptive Mom Blogs in 2016. Their podcast, *Honestly Adoption*, has more than 60,000 subscribers.

Mike and Kristin speak throughout the United States every year with a passion to reach overwhelmed foster and adoptive parents with a message of hope and camaraderie. They are the authors of several books, including *The Adoptive Parent Toolbox* and *The Weary Parent's Guide to Escaping Exhaustion*. Mike is also a featured writer on Disney's *babble.com* and on *The Good Men Project*. His work has also appeared on *Yahoo Parent*, *Your Tango*, *Huffington Post*, *MichaelHyatt.com* and *Goinswriter.com*. Mike and Kristin have been married 18 years and have eight children, all of whom are adopted. They reside in a suburb of Indianapolis, Indiana.

MIKE
BERRY

"I love this book! A wonderful resource for
adoptive and foster parents..."
Jenn Ranter
Founder and Director of Replanted Ministry

CONFESSIONS
of an
Adoptive Parent

Hope and Help from the Trenches of
Foster Care and Adoption

Help and Hope for the Hard Road Ahead

Confessions of an Adoptive Parent is the perfect companion
to the practical advice in this book. Mike Berry knows the
loneliness and isolation you can easily feel in your parenting
role—because he's been there. He is *still* there. Mike's book
will give you the hope and encouragement you so desperately need.

With a refreshing dose of honesty, empathy, and care, you'll
discover you're not alone on your journey and God has a very
special plan for you and your family.

Get More from *Honestly Adoption*

Visit **honestlyadoptionbook.com** for special offers and addi-
tional content not found in the book.